How to Invest
in Canadian Securities

Published by

the Canadian Securities Institute

Canada's leader in investment learning

For

the Investor Learning Centre of Canada

Canada's first not-for-profit organization solely dedicated to educating Canadians about investing.

Canadian Cataloguing in Publication Data

Main entry under title:

How to invest in Canadian securities

Rev. & repr. 1997
Includes bibliographical references and index.
ISBN 0-919796-78-8

1. Investments – Canada.   2. Stock – Canada.   3. Bonds – Canada.
4. Securities – Canada.   I. Canadian Securities Institute.

HG5152.H69 1997   332.63'2'0971   C97-930917-4

First Printing 1970 by the Canadian Securities Institute
Revised and Reprinted 1978, 1984, 1986, 1988, 1994 & 1997

Copyright © 1997 by the Canadian Securities Institute
Published by the Canadian Securities Institute

Printed and bound in Canada

Investor
Learning
Centre
OF CANADA

CANADIAN
SECURITIES
INSTITUTE

Toronto
121 King St. W., 15th Floor, Toronto, ON, M5H 3T9,
Tel. (416) 364-6666 Fax (416) 364-9315

Montreal
1 Place Ville Marie, Suite 2840, Montreal, PQ, H3B 4R4
Tel. (514) 878-3591 Fax (514) 878-2607

Calgary
Suite 2330, 355 - 4th Ave. S. W., Calgary, AB, T2P 0J1
Tel. (403) 262-1791 Fax (403) 265-4603

Vancouver
Suite 1350, P.O. Box 11574, 650 West Georgia St.,
Vancouver, BC, V6B 4N8
Tel. (604) 683-1338 Fax (604) 683-6050

Table of contents

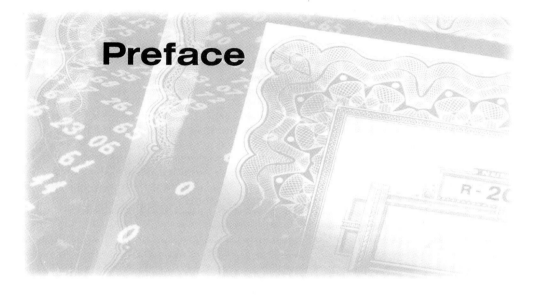

Preface

How to Invest in Canadian Securities is distributed by the Investor Learning Centre of Canada (ILC). The ILC is a not-for-profit organization independent of commercial interests. It was created by the Canadian Securities Institute, Canada's recognized authority in investment learning.

The ILC's role is to give ordinary Canadians easy access to unbiased and authorative information on investing. One of the ILC's major services is the popular seminar series for novice investors called Intelligent Investing. Hundreds across Canada have taken these educational seminars as their first step towards becoming better investors.

This book is the official text for Intelligent Investing. The format is similar to what you would find by being in the seminar room yourself. The main voice in the book is that of Enzo Corelli, the seminar instructor. Enzo has a lot of experience at the front of the classroom. He does his best to present his material in an interesting and lively way.

Enzo also likes to allow time for his students to question his assertions and engage him in discussion. We found that sometimes the discussions reached the noise levels of a futures trading pit at the Chicago Board of Trade! But through the din we were able to make out the voices of two students in particular.

Pat Simcis has her own marketing consulting firm. Now that her business is starting to grow after a couple of slow years, she is in the pleasant quandary of having to decide what to do with the money she has started taking out of the business. Being self-employed, she knows there won't be a fat company pension plan to fall back on during her retirement years. Pat has a good business background, but by her own admission she is a novice investor. She knows she needs to make her money grow but she also can't afford to "play" with it in a haphazard way.

Jason Fleece never did tell us what he does, but he certainly told us a lot about his investing adventures. Jason's been through it all: from asset allocation to zeros, from stocks to swaps, bonds to bull markets, TIPs to bear traps. It was difficult at first to introduce a subject that Jason was not already intimately familiar with (and not just an investing subject). We got the impression that some of Jason's experiences did not produce the most positive of results (and not just his investing experiences). We felt that Jason was at the seminar to find out what he had been doing wrong, although to talk to him, it was usually someone else or something else that had caused his surefire investment schemes to backfire.

We've set the book up so that you can use the Table of Contents to see what will be introduced. Although the book is organized so that the material builds on each chapter, you can also construct your own, smaller book by reading only those chapters that interest you.

We have left side margins for your notes. Our notes are of a twofold nature.

A magnifying glass indicates the seminar's background information.

Material that is more central to the presentation is accompanied by a pencil holder.

We've included a glossary and bibliography at the back of the book. Both of these should help you beyond what is included in our eight chapters.

Happy investing!

Summary

You will find a summary such as this one at the end of each chapter. The preface introduces the structure of this book, which derives from the Investor Learning Centre of Canada's public education seminar program. We have kept the voices of two students in the seminar, Pat Simcis and Jason Fleece. Pat has business experience but knows little about investing. Jason has experience in the markets but knows little about investing. Enzo Corelli, the instructor, will guide them through the basics and not so basics of investing over the course of the seminar. We hope that he does the same for you.

Chapter 1
Investing and the Capital Market

It was five minutes to eight when the instructor arrived in the classroom, but every seat was already full. As he walked to the front of the room, conversations began to die down and thirty pairs of eyes turned towards him...

Good evening. I know we're a few minutes early, but it looks like we have a group of very eager would-be investors here tonight. So let's get started. My name is Enzo Corelli and I'll be your instructor for this course. Over the next few weeks we're going to take a look at some of the most important areas of investing – like how the securities system works; what stocks and bonds are; how to analyse securities; and how to build an investment portfolio. Tonight we'll start off with a general introduction to investing and the capital markets.

Some of you may think you know absolutely nothing about investing. I suspect, however, that you know more than you think. At the very least, you probably know that people can invest in many things, including real estate, securities, stamps, coins and works of art.

In this course we talk about one particular type of investment – securities. Securities can take several forms, including stocks, bonds, mutual funds and options. When you buy and sell securities, you are participating in the capital markets.

Capital

Capital is another word for wealth, such as your savings. The capital market is a mechanism through which people or institutions with money to invest are brought together with those who need money for a variety of purposes.

Excuse me, but who provides capital, and who uses it? And how do securities fit into the picture?

Suppliers

There are two main sources of capital – individuals and institutions. Individuals means people like you and me. Since you're taking this course, I can assume you're interested in becoming an investor. In fact, you almost certainly are already one. You're an investor if you have a bank account, for example. The money you put in the bank is lent to people and businesses. You also may be providing capital directly to businesses or governments through investing in Canada Savings Bonds or other securities.

Another way you may be a source of capital is through institutions. Institutional investors include banks, life insurance companies, pension funds, and mutual funds. If you participate in a company pension plan, for instance, your money is pooled with other peoples' and is then invested in the capital markets. Because of the growth of pension funds and mutual funds in recent years, institutions are an increasingly important source of capital.

Probably everyone in this room here tonight is a supplier of capital. Are any of you users of capital?

I am. My name is Pat Simcis and I run a small consulting business. I have a loan from my bank which I took out for business purposes. And I also have a mortgage for my house from the same bank, so I guess that's another way I use capital.

Users

Absolutely, Pat. You actually represent two types of users – the individual who borrows money for personal reasons, and the business which uses capital to operate and expand. I'll talk more about businesses in a moment. Can anyone here guess what the other main user of capital is?

You bet I can. My name is Jason, and I can tell you that a very large percentage of my personal capital gets used by the government.

I'm sure a lot of people here feel that way. It's true that the government is a major user of capital. However, if you're referring to the government taking money from you in the form of taxes, that's not what I'm focusing on here tonight. I'm talking about governments borrowing money when, believe it or not, the money they get in taxes from us is not enough to cover their expenditures. The three levels of government – federal, provincial and municipal – use the money they borrow for a variety of purposes. They pay for capital projects, like building roads, hospitals, and schools; for social services like welfare; and to pay interest on money they have already borrowed.

Bonds

In general, governments borrow money by issuing debt instruments. Debt instrument is a generic term for securities like bonds and debentures. We're going to talk a lot about these in our third class. But for now, all you need to know is that when you buy a bond, you loan money to the issuer of the bond, such as a government or corporation. The issuer promises to pay this money back to you on a certain date and to pay interest to you in the meantime at regular intervals. A very familiar example is Canada Savings Bonds, which the federal government issues to raise money from the general public.

Governments aren't the only ones who can issue bonds, however – and that brings us literally back to business, another key user of capital. Companies need capital to start up their businesses; to finance day-to-day operations; to renew plant and equipment; and to expand their activities. There are a number of different ways a business can obtain capital, depending on the form the business organization takes.

Pat, you mentioned that you run a small business. If you don't mind me asking, do you own it yourself or do you have partners?

I'm on my own. Which is either a good or bad thing, depending on which day you talk to me.

I used to run a business myself, so I can sympathize. Your type of business is known as a sole proprietorship. One person owns and generally operates it.

The business I ran was a partnership. Three of us owned it and shared the responsibility for managing it.

Business Organization

There is a third form of business organization besides sole proprietorships and partnerships. This is known as the corporation. The corporation differs from the other two in that the owners or shareholders of a corporation have limited liability. They risk only the amount of money they have invested in the company's shares. In a sole proprietorship and partnership there is generally unlimited liability, which means the owners are personally liable to the creditors of the business for any debts.

There are some other advantages to the corporation, such as continuity of existence. That means the company is not necessarily terminated with the death of the owner, as it would be with a sole proprietorship, or with a partnership unless an agreement has been made to the contrary. When the shareholder of a corporation dies, the shares become part of the estate and are passed on to the heirs.

Similarly, shareholders of a public corporation can usually transfer their shares to other investors with relative ease. The ability to buy and sell shares of a corporation is referred to as marketability, and is an attractive feature for many investors.

As well, corporations often can support larger and more complex organizations than can sole proprietorships and partnerships. On the flip side of the coin, proprietorships and partnerships have the advantage of being relatively easy to set up and manage. But they also may find it harder to expand, in part because of the difficulty of raising funds. Just like a proprietorship and a partnership, a corporation can raise funds for its business by borrowing money from banks or retaining profits from the business. Large corporations, however, often have another option – issuing securities like bonds and stocks.

Raising Capital

We talked earlier about how governments issues bonds. Corporations can do much the same thing. By issuing a bond, the company borrows money from investors and is obliged to repay both the principal – the amount borrowed – plus interest – a percentage of the amount borrowed. These amounts must be paid on dates set in the bond contract.

Dividends

Unlike governments, corporations can issue stock as well. The reason companies can issue shares while governments can't is that stock represents ownership. When you buy a share of a company, you become a part-owner. Thus you share in the fortunes of the company, for better or for worse. If you own common stock, for example, the value of your shares may increase if the company does well, and you may also receive dividends. A dividend is money taken out of the company's profits and distributed to shareholders.

If the company begins to do poorly, however, the value of the stock may decline. It can even go to zero! And if the company goes under, shareholders' claim on assets comes behind those of creditors, which includes bondholders. That's why stocks are generally considered riskier than bonds.

We've covered a lot of ground here, so let's take a moment to reflect on where we've been. We've talked about what capital is, and the two main suppliers of capital – individuals and institutions. We've talked about the three main users of capital – individuals, governments and businesses. And we've talked about how governments and businesses can raise capital by issuing securities, such as stocks and bonds.

Now is a good time to look at securities from the investor's perspective. We know why businesses and governments issue securities. The obvious question is why do individuals and institutions buy them. Does anyone have any answers?

To make money, of course.

Investment Objectives

Good answer, Jason. That's certainly the investment objective that springs to most people's minds. But we can be even more specific than that. In general, there are two ways you can earn a return on an investment. First, you can obtain growth of capital. That means an increase in the value of your investment. If you're looking for capital growth, you might buy a common stock that you think is going to increase in price.

Second, you can make money by receiving regular income. Income from a security might be the interest you make on a bond you own.

Another source of income is the fixed dividend you receive when you invest in preferred shares.

In addition to capital growth and income, there is a third investment objective to keep in mind. That's safety of principal. If an investment has guaranteed safety, that means when you invest $1,000, you're sure to get that $1,000 back. If you're primarily seeking safety in an investment, however, you may have to settle for a lesser rate of income and lower potential for capital gain. For example, in Canada the debt instruments issued by the federal government – such as bonds and treasury bills – are considered to have a high degree of safety. For that reason, they generally offer less of a return than higher risk investments like some corporate bonds and stocks. But on the plus side, the return they offer is virtually guaranteed.

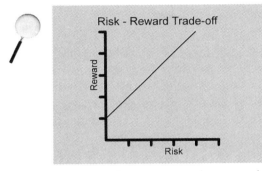

In general, the greater the potential for making money, the greater the risk. As well, securities that offer the potential for capital gain, such as common stocks, are considered higher risk then those that offer income, such as bonds and preferred shares. But be warned that there is a great deal of variation within these categories. All bonds, for example, are not created equal – some may be more risky than others. Likewise for stocks. And some bonds may be riskier than some stocks. If this sounds confusing, relax. In later sessions, we'll learn methods for analysing and comparing the investment value of different stocks and bonds.

Finally there is a fourth major investment consideration – liquidity. A security is liquid if you can buy or sell it on short notice, with little effect on the price. If you might need to get your money out quickly, you need a liquid investment. A very liquid investment is the money in most bank accounts. At the other end of the spectrum, real estate or art objects are often illiquid. That means if you need to sell them quickly, you might have to accept a lower price than you would have received if you had been able to wait longer.

The perfect security would meet all four objectives. It would offer a big increase in capital, a high steady income, guaranteed safety of principal and the ability to be sold at a moment's notice. Unfortunately, there is no perfect security. When you buy a security, you are usually making a trade-off between these four objectives.

Which objectives you favour depends on your financial situation and goals. An elderly widow, for example, might require safety of principal and a regular income. On the other hand, a well-off young executive with few responsibilities might have the income and the risk-taking temperament to try to increase his pool of capital for early retirement. We are going to talk a lot more about financial planning toward the end of the course.

Trading Securities

Up to this point we've talked about two of the major players in the capital markets – the suppliers of capital and the users of capital. And I've outlined how securities are used to transfer capital between suppliers and users. There is one more topic I want to touch on briefly tonight. This has to do with the mechanics of how capital is transferred between suppliers and users – in other words, how securities are traded.

We mentioned earlier that there are many different types of investments. Art is considered an investment by some people, for example. Now if you decide you want to buy art, you know you have to go to a gallery or an auction house. Those are actual, physical places where art is bought and sold.

Securities, on the other hand, aren't quite as tangible as art. By the same token, the securities markets aren't always actual places, although sometimes they are. In eighteenth-century Manhattan, stocks were sold by Wall Street merchants along with their regular merchandise, over the counter. Stock markets with trading floors evolved from this primitive beginning. Nowadays, however, more and more trading floors are being closed, and stocks are being traded through networks of computers. And even in the past, bonds usually weren't traded on floors, but over the telephone and via computer, as they continue to be today. Ironically enough, these computer and telephone-connected markets are called over-the-counter markets, reminiscent of the early days of Wall Street.

So a securities market isn't necessarily a physical place. Instead, it is the meeting place between orders to buy and sell securities. The bond market, for example, is basically the sum of all the orders to buy and sell bonds at any moment in time.

The markets are generally organized and operated by securities firms, such as stock brokers and investment dealers. When a corporation issues new bonds and stocks to raise capital, investment dealers usually are involved in buying and reselling them to the public. The initial sale from corporation to investment dealer takes place in what is known as the primary market.

Later, securities firms help facilitate the buying and selling of stocks and bonds that are already issued and outstanding. This is called the secondary market. There are secondary markets for both bonds and stocks, and they are what we generally think of when we refer to the bond market or the stock market.

In our next session, we are going to look at the securities system and the role of investment firms in greater detail. But I hope I've given you a broad portrait of the capital markets and investing. When you came here tonight, you probably were thinking about the markets from your own point of view as an investor. We're certainly going to spend a lot of time doing that in future sessions. It's worthwhile, however, to remember that as an investor, you are part of a larger process. When you invest, you are supplying capital to individuals, corporations and governments for many important social and economic uses. Your investment may in fact pay off for you in two ways – first, by making you money; and second, by improving our economy and our country as a whole.

See you all next week.

Summary

The investment markets are the meeting place for suppliers of capital, who have surplus funds to invest, and users, who have a need for additional money. Business and government users borrow money by issuing debt securities such as bonds and debentures. Corporations can also raise money by selling shares in themselves, or equity. Financial intermediaries such as investment dealers facilitate the issuing and trading of these securities.

Suppliers choose their investments to satisfy their objectives, which may be capital growth, income or safety. Each of these carries its own levels of risk and reward, which increase at more or less the same rate.

Chapter 2
How the Securities System Works

The role of participants and regulators in the securities system.

Good evening, everyone. I'm glad to see most of you have made it back for our second session.

Our first meeting was quite challenging. We talked about a lot of abstract concepts – such as the capital markets and the role of capital suppliers and users. Tonight we take a more practical approach and look at how the securities markets really work. By the end of the evening, you should have a general idea of what the main organizations in the securities system are, and the roles they play. That's going to set the stage for you to understand the role that you can play in the market.

In our last session, I talked about how a securities market isn't necessarily a physical place. Even when a market does exist physically, like the trading floors of some stock exchanges, people like you and me can't just go there and buy and sell stock. We have to make our trades through intermediaries, generally known as brokers or investment dealers.

Jason, you look like you have the first question of the night.

Well, you say that investors can't trade for themselves. But why can't we? Why do I have to pay a commission to a broker instead of going down to the floor and trading for myself? It's not as if going through a broker is doing anything for my bottom line.

That's a question many people ask. Maybe it seems that the broker you deal with isn't doing a lot for the commission you pay. But you might change your mind if you saw everything that happened behind the scenes.

Say you own some stock in Abacus Inc. and you want to sell it. If you had to go to a trading floor, that would take time. And when you got there, you'd have to find someone willing to buy it from you. You'd have to negotiate the price. And to settle the trade, you'd have to hand over the certificate, and be paid by the buyer. Then you'd have to hope the cheque that the buyer gave you didn't bounce!

Your brokerage firm takes care of all of that for you. It ensures that the trade takes place quickly, fairly, and at the best price possible at the time. It also makes sure that the buyer gets the securities they paid for, and that the seller actually gets paid. Remember that many thousands of securities trades happen in Canada each day. This could not take place efficiently without the work of experienced and trained personnel both at brokerage firms and other industry organizations.

I'm not sure if I've convinced you, Jason. But wait while I spend the next few minutes talking about what brokerage firms do. That might make it clearer.

First, some terminology. I've been using the phrase brokerage firms. These are also referred to as securities firms, investment dealers, stockbrokers, and investment or brokerage houses.

At one time there were meaningful distinctions between some of these terms. It used to be that investment dealers specialized in trading bonds, while brokerage firms focused on trading stocks. The terms also referred to the difference in the way they traded these securities. That is, investment dealers which traded bonds generally acted as principals, while brokers trading stock acted as agents.

The Dealer as Principal

When a firm acts as a dealer or principal, it owns the securities involved in the trade at some point during the transaction. For example, if you called an investment dealer and sold a bond, the dealer would actually buy it from you with its own money. Then the dealer would resell it to another investor. The difference between the price the dealer paid you for the bond and the price it received from the other investor would be its profit or loss on the trade.

The Dealer as Agent

In contrast, when a broker acts as an agent, it brings together two investors who buy and sell from each other. The firm never owns the securities, and is paid a commission for its efforts in arranging the trade.

That's how the terms originated, but the distinctions between them have blurred over time. Now, most of the big securities firms trade both stocks and bonds. And they may act either as a principal or an agent, although not on the same transaction. So when I use the term brokerage firm or investment dealer here tonight, I'm referring to securities firms in general unless I say otherwise.

Types of Firms

I don't mean to suggest, however, that all securities firms do exactly the same type of work. There are many securities firms in Canada, and they differ from each other in many ways. Some have offices across Canada, while others are concentrated in one region of the country. Some have thousands of staff, while other "boutiques" may have just a few employees. Some may offer practically the entire range of services, while others focus on just a few areas. A firm's specialties might be trading securities in a particular industry; dealing only with a certain type of client – for example, large institutions like pension funds; managing portfolios for wealthy individuals; bond or stock trading; unlisted stock trading; or the underwriting of companies in certain sectors.

Securities firms also differ in terms of their ownership. Historically, Canada divided up the financial services industry into four major groups, known as the four pillars. These are the banks, the trust companies, the insurance companies and the securities industry. The government prohibited cross-ownership among the four pillars.

Bangs, Big and Little

In recent years, Canada, like other countries, has embarked on a program of deregulation. You may have heard the term "Big Bang". This was the day in October 1986 when various rules and barriers to competition in the United Kingdom's financial industry were swept away. Less than a year later, on June 30, 1987, Canada had its own Big Bang – sometimes called Little Bang. The traditional four pillar structure began to be dismantled.

This has had considerable impact on the securities industry. Now, the major banks and trust companies in Canada own securities firms, and there are many foreign players as well. But there remain other types of firms in the industry, such as private or publicly-traded independent companies.

Securities firms also vary greatly in terms of the way they are structured internally. A very large, integrated firm might have several different departments, such as sales; underwriting; trading; research; and administration. Sales staff deal with investors, whether large or small. Underwriting specialists work on deals to raise capital for corporations or governments. Traders actually buy and sell stocks and bonds and other securities on behalf of the firm and its clients. The research department is made up of analysts who gather information on companies and issue reports on whether or not they're good buys. And administration covers all the various support functions, such as human resources, finance, compliance, and so on.

With so many different types of firms to choose from, how do I pick one?

Good question – but wrong session. We're going to spend a lot of time looking at that later in the course, during our seventh class.

Right now I want to talk about the main functions of a securities firm. These relate to our discussion in the first session about the users and suppliers of capital. It's the job of the securities industry to bring together those who need capital, such as companies and governments, with those who have capital to supply, such as investors. Securities firms help companies and governments obtain money by issuing securities in the primary market. Then dealers help provide a secondary market in which investors can buy and sell those securities.

Underwriting

Let's take a closer look at the first task we mentioned – underwriting new issues of securities. Underwriting is when an investment dealer, called the underwriter, helps a company or government raise money through new securities. The underwriter's role can basically be either to buy the whole issue of securities and then resell them to investors at a profit, or to act as a broker between the company and investors for a commission. When the underwriter buys the whole issue, this is called a conventional underwriting. When it acts as an agent, its called a "best efforts" underwriting. The underwriting process may also vary depending on whether the security involved is equity, corporate debt or government debt. I'll just take a brief look at the process and some of the differences.

Perhaps the longest and most complicated process takes place when a company is making an Initial Public Offering (IPO) – that is, the company's very first issue of stock to the public at large. A company coming to market for the first time must file a preliminary prospectus with the provincial securities commission. A prospectus is a legal document that describes securities offered for sale to the public, and must be prepared in strict accordance with provincial securities law.

The prospectus should contain full, true and plain disclosure of all material facts related to the issue. Some of the facts that a prospectus should include are details about the underwriting and distribution; a review of the issuing company, its history and operations; risk factors involved in the purchase of the securities; and financial statements.

Material fact

A fact that might reasonably be expected to have a significant effect on the price or value of a security.

When a company files a preliminary prospectus with the securities regulators, it must contain most of this key information, but it might not include the final price at which the securities will be offered to the public. The securities regulator reviews the preliminary prospectus and comments on any gaps in the information presented. The company then files a final prospectus that includes the price and size of the offering. If the regulator accepts the prospectus for filing, the offering can proceed.

It's important to note that by accepting the prospectus for filing, the regulator isn't saying that the securities are a good buy. It is merely saying that the prospectus meets its requirements for disclosing information about the securities.

During this period, the company offering the securities works closely with the investment firms that are underwriting the securities. The investment firms advise the company on such matters as the price and size of the offering, based on their experience and on information the firms gather during a marketing period before the final prospectus is issued.

In a conventional underwriting, the investment firms in the underwriting group will then buy the issue of securities from the company. The company pockets the money, and goes on its way. It is then up to the underwriters to sell the issue of securities to investors. Depending on the size of the issue, the underwriting group may be made up of anywhere from two to eight or nine investment firms. The bigger the issue, the more underwriters are likely to be involved to reduce the risk exposure to any single firm. The underwriting group may also sell part of the issue to other securities firms, known as the Selling Group. This relieves the underwriters from having to sell the entire issue by themselves.

The process I've just described is a traditional, fully-marketed long-form version of underwriting that can take several months. It is most frequently used nowadays for Initial Public Offerings of equity and for subsequent equity or debt issues of companies that aren't large or well known.

Short-form offerings

To speed up the traditional underwriting process, the Canadian securities industry has developed this faster form of underwriting. Called the Prompt Offering Qualification System (POP system), it is used for companies that are established in the market and meet strict requirements for continuous disclosure of material facts. In these cases, companies may not have to prepare a full prospectus because much of the information that would be included in a prospectus is already available and widely known.

Thus in a short-form offering, the company and the underwriters will not go through the lengthy process of issuing a preliminary prospectus and determining through investor road shows the best price for the issue. Instead, a group of securities firms will quickly make a deal with the company to buy the securities issue at an agreed upon price. The underwriters will then resell the securities to investors, bearing the risk that there might not be great interest in the issue or that market conditions might change, leaving them with an overpriced issue to sell. Often there will be no selling group involved in the process, so the underwriting group bears the risk alone.

The Prospectus

All of this might sound complicated, and certainly underwriting is a very specialized field. But from your point of view as an investor, you only need to know a few things. Let's say your Investment Advisor calls you up and offers you the chance to buy some stock that's just being issued. You might want to ask what role your IA's firm is playing in the underwriting. Also, you must by law be given a copy of the prospectus. Generally, every corporation that sells a new issue of securities to the public is required to file a prospectus with the provincial securities regulator. This prospectus also must be delivered to the purchaser.

Securities law usually allows buyers during a distribution the right to withdraw from the agreement to buy the securities within two business days after receiving or being deemed to have received the prospectus. Most provinces also give purchasers the right to rescind or cancel a contract if the prospectus contains a misrepresentation of fact. However, depending on the jurisdiction you're in, you may have to choose between rescinding the contract and the alternative of seeking damages. Consult a lawyer if you find yourself in a situation where this matters to you. But this is very rare.

Okay. Now lets say the ACME company had issued bonds and they have been distributed into the market. You were one of the investors who bought the bonds during the initial distribution. Now you decide you want to sell them. This is where the second key function of the securities dealer comes in – trading in the secondary market.

You call your IA and say that you want to sell your bonds. Bonds are typically traded in and out of a securities firm's own inventory or from the inventory of other firms that specialize in those issues. So your IA will act as a principal in the trade, buying your bonds and then reselling them later to another firm or investor. The IA doesn't charge you commission on the trade. Instead the IA aims to sell your bonds to another investor at a small profit. If you called your IA and wanted to buy a bond, the dealer would sell it to you out of its inventory. Or if it didn't have the bond in inventory, your dealer would buy it from another firm and resell it to you.

Trading in bonds generally takes place in the over-the-counter market. In reality, that means bonds are traded by telephone or computer. The bond market is essentially a giant network of dealers and institutions.

In contrast, the vast majority of stock trading takes place on exchanges. An exchange is a central marketplace where buy and sell orders meet. Usually when you call your broker to buy a stock, the firm won't sell it to you out of its own inventory. Instead, the firm will send your order to the exchange, where it will be matched with a sell order. The exchanges have rules and systems in place to ensure that orders are executed as quickly as possible, at the best possible price.

I should point out that there is also an over-the-counter market for stocks. In Canada, the organized over-the-counter stock market is the Canadian Dealing Network Inc., a subsidiary of The Toronto Stock Exchange. It generally specializes in trading the stocks of junior companies that do not meet the listing requirements of an exchange.

Now let's step back and look for a moment at the role of the securities firms in the market. If you think about it, together the brokerage firms actually "are" the market. This is fairly obvious for the over-the-counter markets, where that market exists as a network of brokers. But it is also true for stock exchanges.

The Stock Exchanges

Although sometimes novice investors think that exchanges are govern-ment bodies, actually a stock exchange is an organization owned and operated by a group of dealers. Dealers that belong to a certain ex-change are known as "member firms".

There are five stock exchanges in Canada. In order of size, they are The Toronto Stock Exchange, the Montreal Exchange, the Vancouver Stock Exchange, the Alberta Stock Exchange and the Winnipeg Stock Exchange.

The Toronto Stock Exchange is by far the largest stock market in the country. It accounts for more than 75% of all stock trading in Canada by value. Montreal is the next largest, and it is also the oldest. Vancouver is next. It operates a fully automated market that is best known for trading emerging ventures. Alberta operates a market largely geared to the needs of junior resource companies from the West. Winnipeg is also a regional exchange, but very little activity takes place on its market.

Although there are differences in the way exchanges operate, most perform a few important roles. These include making sure that trading in its market takes place fairly and efficiently. For example, the exchange operates its trading floor, if it still has one, or else the computer systems through which trading takes place.

Each exchange also sets requirements that companies must meet before they can be listed for trading. Every exchange has its own listing requirements, and these help determine the kind of stocks that are traded on its market. For example, some of the junior firms listed on the Alberta Stock Exchange might not meet the requirements set by, say, The Toronto Stock Exchange or the Montreal Exchange. Companies also must pay fees to list on an exchange, and these too vary depending on the market. An exchange has the right to cancel a listing or delist a company for various reasons, such as bankruptcy or failing to meet the exchange's on-going listing requirements.

Each exchange is also responsible for regulating its market and checking that traders and other market participants follow the exchange's trading rules. Major exchanges also devote considerable resources to market surveillance – watching market activity to detect any unusual price or volume changes in stocks. Detecting unusual changes is important because it may indicate that improper activity, such as illegal insider trading, has taken place. If a rule violation is suspected, the exchanges will follow-up with an investigation.

The SROs

Exchanges also set rules that their members must follow. For that reason, the four major Canadian exchanges and the Investment Dealers Association are known as Self-Regulatory Organizations or SROs. Their rules cover a wide range of areas, including the education and training of member firm employees; the finances of member firms; and members' dealings with their clients. For example, there are strict policies governing the way your Investment Advisor should deal with you. We'll go into greater detail about this in our later session on getting into the market. And not only do they set the rules, the SROs audit their member firms regularly to make sure that the rules are being followed.

Do all exchanges have the same rules?

Not exactly. As I mentioned, each exchange sets its own listing stand-ards and is responsible for seeing that they are met. As well, each exchange has different market regulations, suited to the type of market it operates. There are similarities, no doubt, but there also may be substantial differences.

The SROs, however, do make an effort to coordinate the rules for their members. This is in part because they actually share many members. An investment dealer, for example, might belong to several different exchanges. So it makes sense to have similar rules.

What about regulation of the bond market?

Good question. Just as the stock exchanges monitor their markets, the Investment Dealers Association of Canada monitors the bond and money markets. As an SRO, the IDA regulates its member securities firms, many of which also are members of an exchange.

Enzo, I don't want to be difficult. But I'm having a little bit of trouble with the idea of Self-Regulatory Organizations. Isn't that like ask-ing the fox to guard the hen house?

Perhaps it sounds like that. But there are solid reasons why it's a good idea for the industry to police itself. First of all, as you can imagine, people in the industry are far more knowledgeable about the securities business than anyone outside it. People who know the markets are better able to spot potential problems and make effective rules. As well, self-regulation means the industry bears the high cost of setting rules and enforcing compliance with them. If the government were to take over the many regulatory functions shouldered by exchanges and the IDA, taxpayers would have an even heavier burden.

Also, you mustn't think that the industry can do anything it wants with no thought to the public interest. Look at the diagram (on the next page) showing how the securities industry works. At the very top and centre of the diagram is a box for the provincial commission regulators.

Although the SROs handle much of the day-to-day regulation, they are overseen by provincial government bodies. For example, The Toronto Stock Exchange is overseen by the Ontario Securities Commission. Every by-law and rule must be reviewed by the provincial regulator. And decisions of the Exchange's Board can be appealed to the Commission.

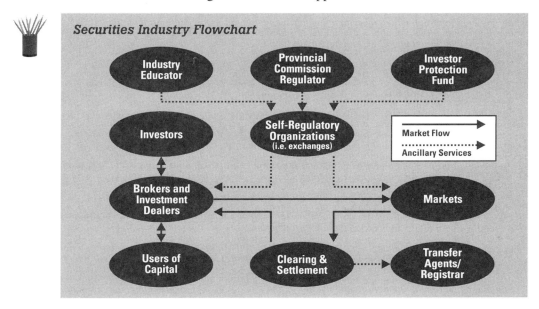

Securities Industry Flowchart

The Regulators

The provincial securities regulators, often called administrators, are also responsible for administering the Securities Acts for their jurisdictions. The general principle underlying Canadian securities legislation is not approving or disapproving the merits of an issue of securities offered for sale. Instead, the administrators focus on requiring full, true and plain disclosure of all relevant facts by those offering securities to the public.

The regulators also require registration of investment dealers and Investment Advisors in order to protect investors. Generally, every firm underwriting or selling securities, and all IAs employed by these firms, must be registered by the securities administrator in the province in which the IA is employed or the securities are sold.

Regulators have the power to suspend or cancel registrations to protect the public interest. They also have powers that put teeth into the securities laws. They can investigate, undertake prosecutions for violations of the acts, conduct hearings, take evidence under oath, seize documents for examination and freeze funds or securities. They have, in fact, many of the powers of the courts.

However, the regulators cannot compel money to be paid back or interfere in the internal disputes of companies' shareholders. But they can halt trading in a security , and deny the right to trade securities in the province. They may also recommend that a charge be laid in the courts should they find that a section of the Securities Act has been violated. That charge might result in a guilty party being fined or imprisoned or both.

You keep saying provincial securities regulators. Isn't the federal government involved?

No. There is no federal securities regulatory body in Canada. That's in contrast to the situation in the U.S. You may have heard of the Securities and Exchange Commission, or SEC, south of the border. The Canadian equivalents are the provincial securities regulators, like the OSC. However, there is a group called the Canadian Securities Administrators, made up of the various provincial commissions and securities administrators. They work together to ensure the provinces' securities regulations are compatible.

But I don't want to give you the impression that the only important organizations in the industry are the SROs and the securities administrators. On the diagram there are other boxes shown too. For example, on the top left a box says Canadian Securities Institute. That's the industry educator, the wonderful people who created the Investor Learning Centre.

Some of you may be wondering how the Institute fits into the industry. Over the years the SROs – the main Canadian exchanges and the Investment Dealers Association – recognized that they all have some functions in common. For example, all of them employ staff who need to be educated about securities. So they decided to jointly sponsor an organization to look after the education of brokers, other members of the industry and the public at large. This is the role of The Canadian Securities Institute.

CIPF

There are a few other organizations that the SROs, and investment dealers who are their members, sponsor together. A very important one is the Canadian Investor Protection Fund, or CIPF. You may have heard about this under its previous name, the National Contingency Fund.

This fund helps protect investors in case their brokerage firm goes under. It works in a similar way to the deposit insurance for banks that many of you probably know about. The CIPF covers losses in a customer's general account of up to $500,000 in cash and securities, with a limit of $60,000 of protection specifically for cash. Say for example that you had $50,000 in cash in your account and $250,000 in stocks and bonds. Even if your brokerage firm went under and was unable to pay you back, all of this would be protected by the industry fund, for a total of $300,000. So you wouldn't lose a dime.

What you're saying sounds good. But are there any hidden catches here about the circumstances in which I'd get reimbursed?

There are no hidden catches. But you do have to remember a few things. First of all, this fund is intended to protect people in case a brokerage firm fails financially. It does not protect you from normal losses in the market. For example, if you invested $100,000 in the stock of Mosquito Farms Inc., and it went bankrupt and the stock went to zero, you might very well lose all of your investment. This fund doesn't protect you from making investment decisions that turn out badly. It only protects you in case the brokerage firm which holds your account and your securities goes under.

Another thing – the Canadian Investor Protection Fund only protects investors who have an account with a member of one of the fund's sponsors. These are the Alberta, Toronto and Vancouver Stock Exchanges, the Montreal Exchange, The Toronto Futures Exchange and the Investment Dealers Association of Canada. If your broker is a member of one of these organizations, your accounts are protected. But not all brokers are members of the IDA or one of these exchanges. So keep this in mind when you start looking for a broker.

Just one more question, Enzo. You said earlier that the exchanges and the IDA aren't government organizations. And the Canadian

Investor Protection Fund is sponsored by the SROs. So this means that when an SRO member goes under, it's not the government who bails out its investors?

That's right. The coverage is paid for by the brokerage firms which sponsor CIPF. The government – meaning the taxpayer – doesn't foot the bill.

I can see that this topic interests a number of you. If you want more information about the Canadian Investor Protection Fund, you can call your IA and ask for a brochure. It goes into detail about how the Fund protects investors.

There's another industry organization I want to talk about briefly. This is the clearing corporation. When a trade takes place, there's a buyer and a seller. The buyer has to pay for the stock, and the seller has to supply the certificate proving ownership of the stock. And this happens thousands of times a day on the markets.

CDS

To keep track of it all, we have a clearing corporation, sometimes called a depository. In Canada, there is one national clearing corporation for stocks and bonds, The Canadian Depository for Securities Limited (CDS). It is used by members of the IDA, the TSE, the Montreal Exchange, the VSE and the ASE, plus by some banks and trust companies.

The work of the clearing corporation is fairly complex and involves extensive use of computers to keep track of all the purchases and sales of securities. As an investor, what you need to know is that you generally have three business days to settle up when you buy or sell stocks and most bonds. That means you have three days to pay for a purchase, and three days to turn in your securities certificates if you are selling.

I own a number of stocks, but no-one ever gave me any certificates!

Most people who own stocks don't actually hold the stock certificates anymore. You own the stock and your account records prove that you do, but you don't have the hassle of keeping the certificates somewhere safe, and making sure they get to your broker quickly when you sell them.

Registration in Street Name

Instead, the securities are registered to your brokerage firm on your behalf, which is called registering the shares in street name. Actually, your broker probably doesn't hold the certificates either. The industry is moving towards paperless settlement. So when a security is transferred from one brokerage firm to another, the certificate doesn't actually move. What moves is an entry in a book showing who owns the stock. And who owes money to pay for the stock.

At the end of each trading day, transactions between investment dealers are added up for every security. So if an investor who deals with investment dealer A bought a stock from an investor at dealer B, the clearing corporation sends a tab to dealer A to pay for the stock, and changes the entry in the book to show that dealer B no longer holds that stock. The process is similar for bond transactions.

It all sounds very complicated, and given the number of trades that happen each day, it is pretty impressive. But it is the fastest, safest way to make sure investors get paid when they sell a security, and receive ownership of a security when they pay for it.

Enzo, I realize I sound like a very suspicious person tonight, but I can't help feeling nervous about the idea of not holding the stock certificate. When I buy something, I want proof I own it.

Some people feel that way. I suppose it's a holdover from the days when people did actually hold stock certificates. But first of all, even without the certificate you do have proof that you own the stock. The proof is in your account statements. And second, think of it as if you were depositing money in the bank. You don't keep cash stuffed in the mattress, do you Pat? Or at least I hope you don't. What you have is a bank statement showing that you have a certain amount of cash in the bank. The bank keeps that cash a lot safer than you could. And it's the same with stocks. Why worry about the certificates getting lost or stolen when the broker will worry for you?

I see your point. And by the way, I only keep a little cash in the mattress – just for emergencies.

That's good. And street name makes it easier for you to arrange for delivery when you eventually sell the shares. In fact, the securities industry around the world is moving away from the traditional use of certificates toward a paperless clearing and settlement system.

Transfer Agent

If you look back at our diagram, you see two boxes we haven't covered yet. One is linked to the clearing and settlement box. That shows transfer agents and registrars. Unlike the other organizations I've been discussing, these are not industry-sponsored groups. A transfer agent is a trust company appointed by a corporation to keep track of its shareholders. The agent records who the shareholders are and where they live. A list of shareholders is important so that shareholders receive any dividends they're entitled to and are notified about meetings where they may be eligible to vote, such as the annual meeting. The registrar double-checks the transfer agent's work and keeps tabs on the status of a company's shares.

That concludes our whirlwind tour of the securities industry in Canada. We've covered a lot of ground tonight, so you can be proud of yourselves. Now we're about to get into the practicalities of investing. This is the fun stuff, but it's also tough. So have a good week, and come back refreshed for our next session.

Summary

This chapter explains the more detailed workings of the securities markets. Investment dealers are one of the key players in these markets. Canadian investment dealers differ in terms of size and areas of specialization. A dealer can function either as a principal or as an agent. A principal owns the securities that it sells, whereas an agent acts as an intermediary between a buyer and seller. One of the dealers' major functions is to underwrite or bring to market new issues of securities. Once an issue has been sold, it will trade on the secondary market, either on an over-the-counter market or a stock exchange.

The Self Regulatory Organizations (SROs) are another major component of the securities system. These are the stock exchanges and the Investment Dealers Association. They establish trading rules and monitor events. The provinces also regulate the markets through their securities commissions.

Other organizations that are part of the system are the Canadian Investor Protection Fund (CIPF), which protects investors against losses caused by the failure of a dealer; the clearing corporation, CDS and the transfer agents and registrars, who keep track of a company's shareholders.

Chapter 3
Bonds, Debentures and the Money Market

The class learns about some of the complexities of the bond market, and Jason sees a world of opportunity arise.

Tonight's talk is about one of the ways companies get the money they need to run their businesses, and how you can help them get it. It's a way that you're probably already familiar with on a personal level, although it works a little bit differently for a corporation.

You get your money in a number of ways. First of all, you earn it by working. Companies do this too – they keep some of their profits and reinvest them in their business.

Or you can go to the bank and borrow it. Companies also rely on borrowed money, except they don't always go to the bank to get it. Borrowing money is a key part of the capitalization process – it is one of the major sources of a company's capital structure. It's interesting to note that governments too are a part of this process. But whereas companies can also raise money by issuing equity, that is, by selling shares in themselves, governments can't. Their money comes primarily from us, in the form of taxes, and from lenders, who may also be us, in the form of government debt instruments such as Canada Savings Bonds, treasury bills and bonds.

Instead of going to the bank, corporations often borrow from individuals or institutions with money to invest. They issue what is essentially an I.O.U., except they call it a bond, debenture, or sometimes other names. What it's called depends on how long it's for, what is going to guarantee that the borrowed money actually does get paid back, and features, if any, that accompany it.

When you buy a bond or debenture you make a loan to the business enterprise or the government body that issued it. The issuer promises to pay this money back to you on the maturity date and in the meantime to pay you interest at set amounts on regular and specified dates, usually semi-annually. Bonds and debentures are issued in Canada by the federal government, by the ten provinces, by municipalities, by government agencies, by business corporations and, occasionally, by religious organizations.

Debt securities issued by municipalities are usually called *debentures*. Traditionally, a debenture is a debt security which is an unsecured promise to pay. That is, there is no property or assets pledged as security for the loan.

This is precisely what a Government of Canada bond is, but custom has established that we speak of Government of Canada bonds, not debentures. Provincial issues may sometimes be designated as bonds and sometimes as debentures. However, securities issued by municipalities and corporate debt issues which are not specifically secured by certain assets are debentures, though sometimes referred to in a general way as bonds.

Over the years a great variety of bonds and debentures has been issued, but tonight we will limit our talk to the more important types of government and corporate money market instruments, bonds and debentures.

Settlement

In the old days, buyers would normally receive a bond certificate after paying for it - known as *settlement* - and hold it in safekeeping while they owned the bond. Nowadays the settlement for most bonds is handled for most banks, trust companies and investment dealers by the same agency that handles stock settlements, The Canadian Depository for Securities Limited, or CDS. If you buy a bond for which a certificate is still available, the settlement procedure is done through a Certificate Based System. If you don't want to receive a certificate, a computerized settlement procedure called a Book Based System is used. Under this system, the certificate is held in the CDS vault and a computerized entry keeps track of your name. The entry will appear on the computer of the bank, trust company or investment dealer with whom you deal as well as in CDS records. Many bonds owned by institutions are held on a book based system and many retail buyers also elect to be on this system.

But how do I decide which bond to buy?

Before you can make that decision you have to know a bit more about what choices are available. Let's start by looking at some of the properties that make bonds similar or different from each other.

ACME Ltd. 8.00% bonds due September 1, 2001 pay $4.00 for every $100 face value on March 1 and September 1 of each year, with the final payment on September 1, 2001.

Bonds maturing:	*Term:*
up to three years	*Short term*
from three to ten years	*medium term*
over ten years	*long term*

Interest

Every bond states on its face the rate of interest which the bond carries. This rate is known as the *coupon rate*. Interest payments are usually made twice a year at six-month intervals and one of the payment dates is the same as the day and month of the maturity date.

Maturity Date

The maturity date is the date on which the amount borrowed is repayable and interest payments end. Bonds usually mature at any time from one to 30 years and sometimes longer. There is no set rule covering the term. However, depending on the time remaining to maturity, the informal guidelines you see here are used in the bond market.

The designation of the term of a bond or debenture depends on the time remaining to maturity, and a debt issue will change its term status as the maturity date approaches. For example, a bond issued in 1985 and due in 2005 was a long term issue with a 20 year term to maturity.

In 1995, the term to maturity became ten years, so the issue is now medium term. In 2002, term to maturity will be three years and the issue is short term.

Callable Bonds

Issuers of bonds frequently reserve the right to pay off the bond before maturity to take advantage of lower interest rates by refunding, or to use accumulated funds to eliminate interest charges. This privilege is known as the *call feature* or *redemption feature* and a bond bearing this clause is known as a callable bond or a redeemable bond. As a rule, the issuer agrees to give 30 days, or more, notice to the bondholder that the bond is being called or redeemed.

Debt which cannot be called before its maturity is known as *non-callable* or *non-redeemable.*

Denominations

The amount the issuer of the bond contracts to pay on maturity is shown on the face of the bond. This is known as the *denomination* or *face value.* The most commonly used denominations are $1,000 or $10,000 and larger denominations to suit the preference of investing institutions such as banks and life insurance companies. Normally, an issue designed for a broad retail market is issued in small denominations. Compound interest Canada Savings Bonds are issued in denominations as low as $100. An issue designed for institutional investors, on the other hand, is made available in denominations reaching into millions of dollars to suit the requirements of the buyer.

Does that mean I can buy $1,000 worth of a government bond? I thought there was a higher minimum than that.

In theory you could buy as little as the lowest denomination issued. But don't confuse denomination with trading unit. A trading unit is the standard trading amount, and it's usually bigger than the denomination. Think of computer diskettes. You use one at a time, so the denomination is one. But you buy them in packages of ten, so that would be their trading unit. You could buy one at a time, but you would probably pay a premium to do so. It's the same with bonds.

Okay, so where do I go to buy one?

The Secondary Market

Investment dealers, in addition to bringing new securities issues to market, perform a second major function by trading in the secondary market and by maintaining an inventory of securities. The principal function of this secondary market is to provide a forum for investors such as you, Pat, to buy previously issued bonds and to sell those they own instead of having to wait for them to mature. An active market allows investors to react to changing economic conditions, not to mention personal circumstances. It also improves primary distribution, since investors can buy new issues and feel confident that they will be able to sell them if need be.

Historically, almost all trading in bonds and debentures in Canada has been conducted on the over-the-counter market, though a few debentures are now traded on the Alberta, Vancouver and Toronto Stock Exchanges. The Canadian bond market is, therefore, an unlisted market and unlisted markets outstrip by far the listed stock markets in dollar volume in Canada.

In 1995 the value of trading on Canada's five stock exchanges was about $256 billion. The Investment Dealers Association estimates that about $10.3 trillion in bond and money market securities traded on the over-the-counter market in the same year.

Participants

Trading in the over-the-counter market is mostly carried on by investment dealers. In a larger investment house the work is divided among several traders. One group handles money market issues, another long-term Government of Canada and provincial bonds, another corporate bonds, and so on.

The sales and trading departments are closely related. Salespeople ask for quotations for securities which clients wish to buy or sell, and traders provide them with this information, as well as quotations on securities owned by the firm or available at another dealer, or "on the street" as this is called.

Spread: the difference between a dealer's cost and selling price.

Prices on the street market are generally determined by negotiation between buying and selling dealers. They will offer to sell securities they own at a slightly higher price than what they paid for them. Another dealer may offer a smaller spread and will presumably make the sale. Where there is a series of bids or offers made in the process of reaching agreement, there is a degree of auction involved. About 100 dealers and a much smaller number of banks and trust companies are active in the street market, which is principally located in Toronto, Montreal and Vancouver. Dealers active in this market are linked to other dealers, banks and large institutional customers by means of the computer systems of five "inter-dealer" bond brokers. Computer screens show the market and size of bid and offering on a wide range of bonds. Dealers can deal through these systems without necessarily knowing the name of the dealer on the other side of the deal until confirmation contracts are exchanged.

The Bank of Canada carries on active open market operations related to its role in the control of the money supply. As a result, the Bank is a major factor in the over-the-counter market for bonds. Traders in Toronto, Montreal, Vancouver and other key centres keep in close touch with Bank of Canada representatives in these cities. The Bank responds only to firm bids and offerings. Dealers are continually in touch with the Bank to test the market by offering or bidding for blocks of Canada bonds.

Market Information

Market information on price, volume, bids and offers is obtained through the inter-dealer computer systems already mentioned or by traders talking to each other. Printed information is also provided by some dealers who issue daily, weekly or monthly quotation sheets, and by the bond quotations supplied by various investment dealers to daily and weekly financial newspapers and wire services.

How easy is it for an investor to trade on the bond market?

The Dealer's Role

An effective secondary market is dependent on a number of dealers who wish to make markets and trade in securities and are prepared to take positions in securities. Trading creates liquidity which is essential for a good secondary market. Relatively high volumes attract additional participation in the market since buyers and sellers can trade, whenever they wish, at competitive prices. If you know that the underwriter will bid for a security you have purchased, you will have more confidence in the security and in the underwriter. By the same token, other dealers will get in touch with the dealer calling a firm market to buy or sell that particular security.

If you decide to sell a bond at a certain price, your IA will advise the bond trader of your offering. The trader will deduct a fraction of a point from this offering price as profit and make a firm bid for the bond. Should you wish to buy bonds, the trader will add a fraction to the price and make a firm offering.

Securities acquired and held by dealers in the course of trading, or as the tag ends of new issues, become part of the firms' *long position* or inventory. Inventory is sometimes acquired as a result of a new issue moving slowly, or as a service to clients who wish to dispose of securities.

The size of the inventory carried is usually determined by the dealer's assessment of the general market at the time and by its need to maintain reserves for possible future commitments. It is also related to the dealer's own capital because of the IDA's minimum capital regulations which require the margining of inventory held.

Another function of an underwriting dealer is to act as trading agent and help an issuing company fulfil its sinking fund or purchase fund obligations. This gives such a dealer an advantage in calling markets in securities it has underwritten for the issuing company. The dealer is enabled to maintain an orderly market in these securities which in turn will facilitate further new issues.

Purpose of a Bond Trading Department

The purpose and function of a bond trading department is:

- to assist in the original offerings of securities to the public by absorbing securities taken in exchange for new issues, and by maintaining marketability for new issues to the greatest extent possible during and following original offerings;

- to make or obtain competitive bids on securities and to offer or obtain securities on a competitive basis for the investor or speculator, thereby making it possible for the seller or buyer to complete transactions with a minimum of delay;

- to manage the investment dealer's own security position or inventory;

- to gain, particularly by contact with other bond dealers, relevant information related to the bond market, which will help in trading or in allowing new underwritings to be properly priced.

If this is an over-the-counter market, and there's no physical location, how is it policed?

Regulation of Bond Trading

The details and mechanics of the unlisted, high-grade market in Canada are regulated by the Investment Dealers Association. The rules cover all major aspects of trading: trading practices, including full details of sizes to be traded, trading units and rules on delivery practices, including rules on regular delivery, accrued interest and good delivery, buy-ins, and general regulations concerned with the trading and delivery of bonds, debentures and unlisted stocks.

When you buy or sell bonds, accrued interest is included in the total amount. Interest accrues from the last interest payment date up to the settlement date. As the seller, you would receive this amount from the buyer. The buyer would regain this interest at the next interest payment date or if they sell the bond in the meantime.

Bonds which are bought or sold without accrued interest are said to have been traded flat.

Accrued interest

On June 16 you buy $20,000 of 8.00% ACME Ltd. bonds due Sept. 1, 2001. Interest accrues from March 2 (the day after the most recent semi-annual interest date) to June 19 (settlement date – three business days after the trade date). Number of days of accrued interest:

March 2-31	*30 days*
April	*30 days*
May	*31 days*
June	*19 days*
TOTAL	*110 days*

Accrued interest calculation:

$$\frac{\$20,000}{1} \quad X \quad \frac{8.00}{100} \quad X \quad \frac{110}{365} \quad = \quad \$482.19$$

Do I pay tax on this accrued interest?

Taxation of Bond Income

If you are the seller then yes, you do. For the buyer, total accrued interest paid on the purchase of bonds or debentures is a recognized deduction from total interest received. You should preserve contract notes covering purchases and sales of bonds so that accurate income tax returns regarding accrued interest can be made.

If I received an interest payment in February, do I have to figure out how much of the money was earned in the previous year and how much in the current year? That sounds like a pain.

Fortunately not. You are deemed to receive the interest from a fully registered bond as of the date of the interest cheque.

In general, Canadian tax laws provide that interest income from debt securities is taxed as income at your personal tax rate. Interest income has no equivalent to the federal Dividend Tax Credit which gives you a break on dividends from stocks.

What if I had a profit from selling a bond?

Sale or redemption of a bond can result in a taxable capital gain or allowable capital loss. Your gain or loss would be the difference between the proceeds received on the sale and the adjusted cost base. If you were selling a treasury bill though, Pat, the price gain would be regarded as interest income, which is taxed at your personal tax rate.

What is an adjusted cost base?

This is either the amount that you paid for a bond, or it's the weighted average price of a bond bought at different prices on different dates.

Bonds trading significantly below par are particularly desirable for most high tax-bracket individuals since a substantial portion of their return is regarded as capital gains, only 75% of which is taxable. The advantage is greater for high tax-bracket individuals than for others, since their tax rate is higher. The capital gains rate is not normally applicable to "traders" who are in and out of the market all the time. Their gains are regarded as a regular part of their income and taxed as such.

Adjusted Cost Base

Purchase Date	Face Value	Price	Cost
June 1	$10,000	96	9,600
July 2	$5,000	98	4,900
Total	$15,000		14,500
Adjusted Cost Base		96.67	

What if I don't sell my bond? How do I figure out how much it's making for me?

Calculating Bond Yields

What you're asking is how to calculate the bond's yield. This is a large topic and we have to start with a couple of definitions.

A $10,000 bond which is purchased for $10,000, plus accrued interest, is said to have been bought *at par.* A bond purchased for less than par is said to have been bought at a *discount,* while a bond purchased for more than par is said to have been bought at *a premium.*

We suggest you have a calculator handy while reading the next ten pages.

Yield to the investment industry is the annual income from an investment expressed as a percentage of the cost or market price. In the case of stocks, yield is simply the indicated annual dividend expressed as a percentage of the market price. But with most bonds, this relationship is complicated by the assumption that you will be repaid the par value of your investment at maturity.

Unlike a stock yield, a bond yield not only reflects your return in the form of income, but also makes allowance for any capital gain or loss realized when the bond matures. Consequently, a bond yield to maturity is made up partly of income and partly of capital gain or loss.

Suppose you bought at par an 8% $5,000 bond maturing in six years. Let's figure out the return or yield you would get from it.

First, what income would you receive?

$400 a year!

That's right. Next: what capital gain or loss would you get?

The usual for me: none!

Also correct, if you held it to maturity or sold it at par. The reason is that the bonds were bought at par and will be paid off at par on maturity, so no gain or loss results. The gross or pre-tax return would then be

$$\frac{\$8 \text{ (income)}}{\$100 \text{ (purchase price)}} \quad X \quad 100 \quad = \quad 8\%$$

Why did you use those numbers? We just said that the income would be $400, not $8.

When we do a yield calculation we always do it in terms of one year and for $100 face value – how much income did you get for each $100 face value? That's the numerator. How much did you pay for each $100 face value? That's the denominator.

Let's take another example. Suppose the same 8% $5,000 bond was bought at a discount, say for 94. The income received per $100 face value is the same: $8. What capital gain or loss would you get?

A six dollar gain.

Yes, but since we're looking at the income received in one year, we should do the same for the gain. Six dollars over a six-year period is $1 per annum. In this case your annual pre-tax return is:

$ 8   income
$ 1   capital gain
$ 9   total

So, the pre-tax yield is: $\dfrac{9}{94} \quad X \quad 100 \quad = \quad 9.57\%$

In practice it has been found that an answer closer to the correct answer can be obtained by using the average of the purchase price and redemption price at maturity as the divisor:

$$\frac{94 + 100}{2} \quad = \quad 97$$

so: $\dfrac{9}{97} \quad X \quad 100 \quad = \quad 9.28\%$

This is why this yield calculation is called the average purchase/redemption price method.

Rough yield = $\dfrac{coupon \ + \ annual \ capital \ gain/loss}{average \ of \ purchase \ \& \ redemption \ prices}$

Isn't there a shorter name?

In fact there is. It's also known as a rough yield calculation.

Most bonds pay interest twice a year. But there is one type of bond that does not. In fact, it pays no interest at all. Not only that – but you have to pay tax on the interest that you didn't receive.

This sounds like a great type of bond! Why would anyone buy it?

So far I've only told you the bad news. The good news is that it lets you lock in a compounded reinvestment rate, and so avoid one of the major risks of bonds: the reinvestment risk.

Hey, slow down! You've lost me.

We are getting a bit ahead of ourselves. Let's start at the beginning.

Strip Bonds

I've started to describe a zero-coupon or strip bond. In order to understand strip bonds, it helps to think of a regular bond as a series of payments promised to the holder. Let's go back to our $5,000 8% six-year bond. It consists of 12 twice-yearly $200 payments for the next six years, and a $5,000 payment at the end of that time. When we buy the bond, we're buying all those promises to pay.

Now imagine that those 13 payments were sold individually.

Do you mean that I could buy one $200 coupon by itself?

That's right. And you would be buying what we call a zero coupon bond.

Zeros first appeared in Canada in 1982. They are usually created by a dealer acquiring a block of existing high quality federal or provincial government bonds and then physically separating the individual coupons from the bond certificate. Each coupon is then sold separately at significant discounts to its face value. The certificate itself, which is now called the residue, representing the principal amount, is also sold separately. In effect it too becomes a zero coupon bond.

Holders of strip bonds receive no interest payments. Instead, the bonds are purchased at a discount at a price that will result in a certain compounded rate of return. Given a specified interest rate and term to maturity, a Present Value Factor table can be used to determine an appropriate price. For example, if you wanted to receive a compounded rate of return of 8% on one of our coupons due in six years with a face value of $200, you would pay $0.63 per $1.00 face value, or (0.63 X 200) $126. In return for giving up the regular cash flow that semi-annual interest payments provide, you lock in a compounded rate of return.

Present Value Factor tables – single payments

The present value of an isolated $1 payment due in X years time is calculated using the following present value (or discount) rates (rounded to 3 decimals):

Year	5%	8%	10%	12%	Year	5%	8%	10%	12%
1	.952	.926	.909	.893	11	.585	.429	.350	.287
2	.907	.857	.826	.797	12	.557	.397	.319	.257
3	.864	.794	.751	.712	13	.530	.368	.290	.229
4	.823	.735	.683	.636	14	.505	.341	.263	.205
5	.784	.681	.621	.567	15	.481	.315	.239	.183
6	.746	.630	.564	.507	16	.458	.292	.218	.163
7	.711	.584	.513	.452	17	.436	.270	.198	.146
8	.677	.540	.467	.404	18	.416	.250	.180	.130
9	.645	.500	.424	.361	19	.396	.232	.164	.116
10	.614	.463	.386	.322	20	.377	.215	.149	.104

I've always meant to ask: what is compound interest?

Compound Interest

Compound interest is interest paid on interest. The interest that the zero coupon bond *doesn't* pay you is added to the principal. This larger amount then earns interest, which in turn accumulates and earns interest. The present value table uses compound interest calculations. If you take the $0.63 from the table and add 8%, what do you get?

$0.68.

Which is the 8%, five-year number.

And adding 8% to that will give you $0.735, the next number up the chart. If you keep adding 8% you will get back to the $1.00 at the top of the chart. That's compounding. It can make your money grow at a rapid rate; some people refer to "the magic of compounding". Compound interest can have a significant effect on an investment: have a look at the 12% column. What is the present value of a one dollar payment due in six years?

It says .507.

Yes. This means that at 12%, you could invest 50.7 cents and it would be worth a dollar in six years. Your money would have doubled in that time period.

Not bad! Where do I get one?

Keep in mind that you have to get a return of 12% for your money to double in that time period. That would be hard to do right now, although in the early 1980s it would have been easy. As well, there are some other characteristics of strips that you should consider before purchasing them. The securities administrators agree, because they require that first-time purchasers be given a special Purchase Circular, or Information Statement. The Circular must address some of the ways in which zeros differ from other bonds. Among these are price volatility, income tax consequences, and extent of the secondary market.

I'd like to focus on the price volatility aspect, because it can show us a lot about factors that affect the price movements of all bonds. First, let's dispose of the other areas.

As I mentioned earlier, you must declare income from these bonds every year even though you receive no interest payments. This is called deemed interest.

How do you know how much interest to report if you didn't actually receive any?

Taxation of Zeros

Our present value table can help us here. Let's say you buy the $5,000 bond residue from our example. It matures in six years. You might pay $3,150 for it. If you divide 3,150 by 5,000 you will see that our discount factor is .63, which appears in the six year row in the 8% column.

A year later, with five years until maturity, the discount rate is .681, and the value of the residue should be .681 times 5,000, or $3,405. The theoretical value of the residue has increased from $3,150 to $3,405, or $255. You would report $255 of interest income on your tax return.

Extent of the Secondary Market

The administrators want investors to realize that zeros trade on the over-the-counter market like other bonds. There is no guarantee that there will be a healthy market for any particular coupon. However, the market has grown dramatically in the 1990s, so it is no longer likely that investors will not be able to trade their coupons.

Price Volatility

The administrators also want you to know that a zero coupon bond will be more volatile than a conventional bond with the same term and risk. Let's see why it would be.

Let's say you buy a conventional $5,000 8% bond due in six years. What will you end up getting from the issuer if you hold the bond until maturity?

Well, hopefully, my $5,000 principal.

Yes; what else?

What about all those interest payments? 8% of $5,000 is $400; six years of payments is $2,400.

Exactly. So in fact you're getting $7,400 from the issuer: the $5,000 principal and the $2,400 interest.

Now, what would be a safer way to get your money; a bit at a time, spread out over the five years; or all at once, at the end?

A bird in the hand...

Right – a regular bond gives you your money back in instalments. In our example, the interest payments represent 32.4% of the total, and you would get them semi-annually over the five years.

A zero makes you wait until maturity before any of your money is returned. You paid $3,150 for the $5,000 residue of our sample bond. You would not see any money until the six-year mark, and then you would see it all. This is clearly the more risky process. As a result zeros tend to be more volatile traders.

There is a technical name for what we are talking about – bond analysts would call it *duration*. Duration is the average term of all the bond payments – coupons and principal – weighted by the amount of the payment and its present value. Duration for a zero is simple: since there is only one payment, its duration is the same as its term. The duration of our 8% six year bond is a little more complicated to figure out...

But it will be less than six years, because you're getting some of your money back along the way: to be exact, 29.7% of it, not 32.4% – the payment date for the final $200 coupon is at maturity, along with the $5,000 principal.

Right you are! Jason, you have the makings of a bond analyst. But back to duration – the duration of our bond is 4.88 years.

So tell me again what that 4.88 years signifies.

In simple terms, that figure is the average amount of time you will wait to get your money back.

But if I start getting my money back with the first coupon payment six months from now, get a number of evenly spaced payments after that, and get the last payment of principal...

...Along with that final coupon payment...

Yes, Jason, how could I forget? And get the last payments when the bond matures in six years, why would the duration not be 3.25 years, which is the average time of my 12 payments?

That would be true if duration calculations did not also consider the amount and present value of each payment. Your last payment is by far the largest, since it includes the principal, so even though its present value factor is the smallest, it still ends up weighting the scale past the natural mid-point.

But back to volatility: there is also a mathematical reason zeros have wider price fluctuations. Let's look at our 8% six-year bond again. Assume a year has gone by, and interest rates are still at 8%. What would our bond be priced at?

$$Yield = \frac{what\ you\ get}{what\ you\ pay} \qquad 8\% = \frac{8}{?}$$

If it has an 8% coupon, then it would have to be at 100 to yield 8%.

Exactly. Bonds will always move in price to reflect current interest rates. Since the coupon is fixed, it is the price that must change to keep the yield in line with changes in rates.

What if rates then rose to 9%?

I don't think I would want to buy that bond if it was only yielding 8%. I could buy a newly issued one and get 9%.

Unless our bond changed its price so that it yielded 9%; then you might feel differently. If it was priced at less than 100, its yield would increase.

In order to get 9%, you would have to get some of your return in the form of a capital gain.

A bond purchased at par provides a yield rate identical with the coupon rate on the bond.

A bond purchased at a discount provides a yield rate higher than the coupon rate.

A bond purchased at a premium provides a yield rate lower than the coupon rate.

You would have to get an extra 1% as a capital gain, since the coupon itself was giving you 8%.

More or less. Keep that in mind for later when we talk about how the coupon affects volatility: the more of the yield that is obtained through the coupon, the less of it that has to be realized through a price change.

You could get that capital gain if you bought the bond at less than par and it matured at par.

But at what price?

There are formulas that will tell you the price you would pay for an 8% six-year bond so that your yield would be 9%, or, for that matter, the price you would pay for any bond to give you a particular yield. These formulas calculate the net present value of each coupon and the principal, using whatever interest rate you specify. They then add up all these values, which gives you the total present worth of the bond. Dividing by the face value gives you a price relative to 100.

As you can see by our chart, the net present value of all the bond's payments is $4,815.21. That's 96.3% of face value, so to get a 9% yield from that bond, you would have to buy it at 96.30.

Pricing at $5,000 8% six-year bond when interest rates are at 9%.

Payments Face Value	Term	Discount Rate (rounded)	Present Value
200	0.5	0.958	191.57
200	1.0	0.917	183.49
200	1.5	0.879	175.75
200	2.0	0.842	168.34
200	2.5	0.806	161.24
200	3.0	0.772	154.44
200	3.5	0.740	147.92
200	4.0	0.708	141.69
200	4.5	0.679	135.71
200	5.0	0.650	129.99
200	5.5	0.623	124.50
200	6.0	0.596	119.25
5,000	6.0	0.596	2,981.34
Total			4,815.21

$4,815.21 is 96.30% of the $5,000 face value: the bond would be priced at 96.30.

It looks like we've taken our poor 8% bond and turned it into 13 zero coupon bonds!

Well, don't forget that when you buy a bond you are buying a series of future payments, each one of which resembles a zero coupon bond. And bonds are priced in the same way as zeros, except they have more than one component to deal with.

So if I pay 96.30 for this bond, or $4,815 for the $5,000 face value, I'll be getting a 9% yield?

The rough yield calculation should tell us that. The numerator would be the $8 coupon plus the annual gain on the price change from 96.30 to 100.

The gain is $3.70, which is $0.617 annually. So our numerator would be $8.617.

The denominator would be the average of 100 and 96.30. That's 98.15.

So our calculation would look like this:

$$\frac{8.617}{98.15} \quad X \quad 100 \quad = \quad 8.78\%$$

*Now I see why they call it a **rough** yield calculation.*

It's actually not bad when you consider the amount of work involved, compared to what we had to do using present value.

Now let's look at the effect an interest rate change would have on a zero coupon bond.

Remember we talked about buying the $5,000 residue at 63, which would give us an 8% yield over six years. What if interest rates went to 9%?

The discount rate for a six-year term at 9% is .596; so the residue would drop to 59.60 from 63.

So on a percentage basis, our zero suffered more than the regular bond from a 1% rise in rates. The zero went down 5.40%, whereas in dropping from 100 to 96.30, the regular bond lost 3.70%. The zero lost 1.7% more of its value.

Way back when we started talking about zeros, you said that they let you avoid reinvestment risk. What did you mean?

With a regular bond, you get interest payments every six months. Having to reinvest those payments can be a problem.

Why is that a problem? I wouldn't mind.

We all like the thought of getting money regularly. But think of a portfolio manager with millions of dollars in bonds. The coupon payments would be substantial. In fact, on a long-term bond, the coupon payments far exceed the principal. And whatever the coupon rate, the manager will only be able to reinvest the payments at the going rate at the time they are received. Yet that reinvestment rate is a huge factor in the bond's total return.

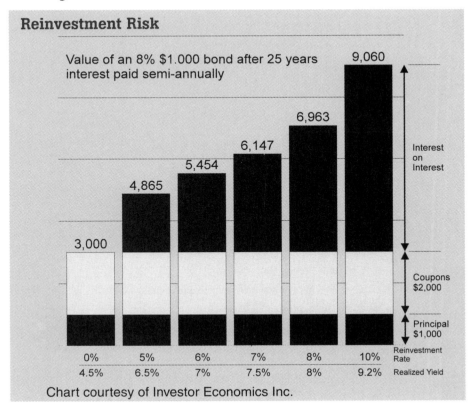

Reinvestment Risk

Value of an 8% $1.000 bond after 25 years interest paid semi-annually

Reinvestment Rate	0%	5%	6%	7%	8%	10%
Realized Yield	4.5%	6.5%	7%	7.5%	8%	9.2%

Values: 3,000 / 4,865 / 5,454 / 6,147 / 6,963 / 9,060

Interest on Interest

Coupons $2,000

Principal $1,000

Chart courtesy of Investor Economics Inc.

Since zero coupon bonds do not have interest payments, there is nothing to reinvest. When you buy the bond, you've already locked in the rate at which the money will compound. You know how much you will end up with. A regular bond doesn't give you that luxury because you never know the rate at which you can reinvest the coupon proceeds.

For someone who needs to know exactly what their investment will be worth a few years down the road, strip bonds seem like a great thing. But the idea of paying taxes on money you didn't even receive...

Strip bonds aren't for everyone. They do present problems if you hold them in a taxable account.

Do I have a choice?

In fact you do. You can hold strip bonds in a self-directed RRSP. In fact they're quite well suited for RRSPs. Investment returns aren't taxed inside an RRSP, so that eliminates the zero coupon tax problem. And as well, your RRSP investments shouldn't be geared to current income, since hopefully you're not going to touch the money at least until you retire. You should be more concerned with their value in the future than how much income they generate this year.

That sounds like a job for a strip bond.

It is. No unneeded income, no reinvestment risk, a known future value – it's a perfect fit. But we'll talk more about RRSPs when we get to financial planning.

We've talked a lot about the price movements of strip bonds. What about regular bonds?

Actually much of our strip bond discussion will help us now when we look at regular bonds.

Bond Price Movements

Bond prices and yields in the secondary market are determined by:
- The level of interest rates
- The credit rating of the issuer
- The term to maturity of the issue

- The coupon rate of the issue
- Features of the issue

Let's look at these one at a time.

The Level of Interest Rates

When interest rates rise, bond prices as a group fall. When interest rates fall, bond prices as a group rise. Such price movements are required to bring bond yields into line with current interest rates, given that the coupon rates do not change. Bond prices are, therefore, subject to the day-to-day fluctuation of the market place.

The Credit Rating of the Issuer

The stronger the financial position of the borrower and the higher its credit rating, the more favourable are the terms at which it can borrow. For example, the Government of Canada can borrow at lower cost than a provincial government, and a provincial government can borrow at lower cost than most municipalities. Similarly, a well-known established company can borrow on more favourable terms than a small business.

The Term to Maturity of the Issue

Traditionally, money borrowed for long periods is more costly than money borrowed for short periods. This is logical because more things can happen over a 20 year period to endanger the repayment of the debt than can happen in one year. Investors therefore require a higher yield to compensate for the higher risk.

A long-term bond also provides another type of risk not present in a short-term bond. This is the exposure to inflation, the great enemy of bonds.

 I know this is pretty basic, but what exactly is inflation? Everybody talks about it, but I get the feeling not everybody knows what it really is.

You're probably right. I'm sure you've been in stores where the new higher prices are blamed on "inflation", even when the inflation rate is around 1%. Inflation is the reduction in the purchasing power of money. Ten years ago a dollar would buy you a pound of butter. Now it will buy you a third of a pound. The butter hasn't changed; the value of your dollar has.

It seems inevitable that the value of money will shrink over time; the question is, at what rate. The Consumer Price Index, or CPI, is the measure we use to track inflation. It is calculated by adding up the price of a group of household goods. The total price in 1986 was set at 100, and all other years are set relative to that. So the CPI has an absolute number, but it is more commonly compared to what it was last year, so we can see the percentage change.

All those annual increases add up over time. So the longer you have to wait to get your money back, the more chance inflation has to erode its value.

Consumer Price Index

Year	Level	Percentage Change	Year	Level	Percentage Change
1980	67.2	10.2	1987	104.4	4.4
1981	75.5	12.4	1988	108.6	4.0
1982	83.7	10.9	1989	114.0	5.0
1983	88.5	5.7	1990	119.5	4.8
1984	92.4	4.4	1991	126.2	5.6
1985	96.0	3.9	1992	128.1	1.5
1986	100.0	4.2	1993	130.2	1.6

But coupon payments give you some of your money back every year.

That's right. And the size of the coupon affects the rate at which you get your money. This is where duration becomes such an important concept, because it takes coupon payments into account. We should really say, the longer the duration, the greater the inflation risk. Instead, we talk about the longer term. The assumption is that for the most part longer-term bonds have longer durations.

We expect, then, that owing to these risks, a long-term bond will have a higher yield than a short-term bond. Bond analysts use a graph called a yield curve to represent the yields of bonds with differing terms. To compare apples to apples, a yield curve will only use bonds of one issuer, such as the Government of Canada.

Yield Curve

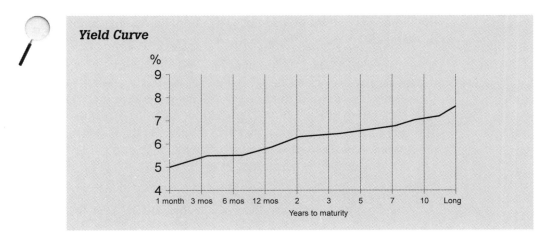

I would expect that long-term bonds would react more strongly to interest rate changes than short-term ones, because the change in their present value would be greater.

You would be right. Have a look at our present value chart. If rates rise from 8% to 10%, the present value of $1 due in six years drops from $0.63 to $0.564, or 10.5%. But at ten years, the drop is from $0.463 to $0.386, or 16.6%. The longer term accentuates the price adjustment.

We can see the same effect illustrated in this chart.

The most volatile bond combines long term and low coupon. The least volatile has a short term and high coupon.

Market Price Volatility

Bond	10%, 5 year	Zero, 5 year	10%, 20 year	Zero, 20 year
Price	100	61.39	100	14.20
Yield	10	10	10	10
Price with rate at 7%	112.47	70.89	132.03	25.26
% change	+12.47	+15.47	+32.03	+77.89
Price with rate at 13%	89.22	53.27	78.78	8.05
% change	-10.78	-13.23	-21.22	-43.30

Just as I would have suspected.

The Coupon Rate of the Issue

As we have seen, a bond with a high coupon will trade at a higher price and with less volatility than a similar bond with a low coupon. The greater the portion of the overall yield that you receive over the life of the bond, through the semi-annual coupon payments, the lower the risk and therefore the higher the price.

Features of the Issue

Certain features of a debt issue, such as convertibility or a call provision, can affect its market price. For example, if a debt issue has a sinking fund or purchase fund feature, the fund's market activities may influence the issue's market price. When the fund bids for the issue to retire whatever is bought for sinking or purchase fund purposes, the issue's market price could be favourably affected.

How can I benefit from all these price characteristics of various bonds?

The Yield Curve and Bond Switching

This is what bond traders spend their day worrying about. Not only do bond prices and yields fluctuate but also the relationship between short-term and long-term bond yields tends to fluctuate. This latter relationship is easily seen in a yield curve, which continually changes. Because of changing prices and yields as well as changing yield curves, there are often many bond switching opportunities in bond portfolios.

Here is a summary of possible benefits from switches of bonds.

Net Yield Improvement

There may be opportunities to improve yield after tax without adversely affecting quality. For example, a high tax bracket investor will be better off in deep discount bonds than in high coupon bonds even if the gross yield is the same, because the tax rate on the discount portion of the yield will be based on the capital gains rate and hence lower. On the other hand, a low tax bracket investor would be better off in a high coupon bond.

Term Extension or Reduction

There will be many opportunities in this area due to changing yield curves and to changing requirements.

Improvement in Credit

This involves a switch to bonds with a better quality credit. This is particularly possible in corporate bonds, where the prospects for entire industries or particular companies can change radically and sometimes quickly.

Portfolio Diversification

Price changes in a portfolio, or the impact of new cash income or cash requirements can necessitate reviewing the portfolio. It may need to be further diversified to ensure that risks are spread and not concentrated.

Cash Take-outs

These are possible when the proceeds from sale of a bond exceed the cost of the bond purchased with the proceeds. Sometimes it is possible to do this without adversely affecting yield or quality.

Bond Switching Hints

The differing behaviour of bonds with varying coupons and terms enables the astute bond investor to take advantage of interest rate swings by either shortening or lengthening the average term of the bond portfolio. This approach is implemented by holding a portion of the bond portfolio in long-term low coupon bonds when yields are in the downward phase of the interest rate cycle and bond prices are rising. The investor then reverses the position when yields rise and bond prices fall.

By doing this successfully, a bond investor will make an additional pre-tax return over the average coupon income. However, success will depend on ability to forecast the bond market correctly.

Technical factors related to supply and demand, yield and price spreads for various types of bonds will often make bond switches attractive.

Sinking fund or purchase fund operations often cause temporary distortions in the market that make certain bond switches advantageous.

A sharp rise in the underlying common stock of a convertible debt issue or a debt issue with warrants attached could result in the debt issue selling at a substantial premium above par. In such an instance, a switch to another debt issue could prove advantageous.

The market price of a convertible debt issue might decline once a previously indicated date for a change in conversion terms had passed. In such an instance an opportunity for a bond switch might present itself.

Switches for these and other reasons are a fascinating and continuing aspect of portfolio management.

How do I find out the price of a particular bond?

Reading Bond Quotations

You turn to the bond quote section of the paper. A typical bond or debenture quotation in a newspaper might look like this:

Issue	Coupon rate	Maturity	Bid	Ask
ABC Company	11½%	1 July/97	99.25	99.75

This quotation would mean that, at the time reported, an 11«% coupon bond or debenture of ABC Company which matures on July 1, 1997 could be sold for $992.50 and bought at $997.50 per $1,000 face or principal amount. Some financial newspapers publish a single price for the bond or debenture, which may be the bid price, the midpoint between the final bid and ask quote for the day, or a price which is an estimate at current interest rate levels. Convertible issues are usually marked by an asterisk or grouped together separately.

If the ABC Company debenture was extendible it would usually appear in the financial pages as follows:

Issue	Coupon rate	Maturity	Bid	Ask
ABC Company	11½%	1 July/97/02	99.25	99.75

The holder of this debenture would have the option of extending the term of the debenture from July 1, 1997 to July 1, 2002.

Retractables are generally indicated in the following manner:

Issue	Coupon rate	Maturity	Bid	Ask
ABC Company	11½%	1 July/02/97	99.25	99.75

The holder of this bond would be able to redeem the bond on July 1, 1997 instead of holding it to July 1, 2002.

Did I miss something?

Extendible and Retractable Bonds

Yes Pat – I should tell you about extendibles and retractables. Extendible bonds and debentures are usually issued with a short maturity term but with the option for the holder to extend the debt for an additional term at the same or slightly higher rate of interest. In effect, the extendible bondholder can extend the maturity of the bond from short to mid or long term.

Retractable bonds are the opposite to extendible bonds. They are issued with a long maturity term but with the option for the holder to turn in the bond for redemption at par several years sooner. In effect, the retractable bondholder can retract or pull back the maturity of the bond from a long to a shorter term date.

Buyers are attracted by the flexibility of extendible and retractable issues, and as a result they sell at a lower yield than straight issues. One of the factors you must consider when choosing a bond term is where you think interest rates are going. If you think they're going up, you would choose a short-term bond so as not to get stuck with today's issue when the ones coming out next year will have more attractive rates. If you think interest rates are headed down, you would want a longer-term bond, to lock in today's higher rates. Extendibles and retractables let you hedge your bets; you can decide later on the term.

You make your decision during the *election period,* which normally lasts for six months. The election period normally occurs from one year to six months before the first maturity date. With extendibles, you use this period to notify the appropriate trustee or agent of the debt issuer whether you wish to extend the term of the bond or allow it to mature on the earlier date. If you take no action, the bond automatically matures on the earlier date. With retractables, you must take action if you want to exercise the retraction option during this period; if you do nothing, the debt automatically remains long term.

Extendible and retractable issues are sometimes referred to as *variable maturity* or *exchangeable* debt. The flexibility inherent in these features has made this type of debt quite popular with investors. This flexibility is not an attractive feature for issuers, since they do not know in advance whether the securities will be held for the shorter or the longer maturity option.

Classifying Bonds

Generally speaking, corporate bonds may be classified by two methods. One way is to group bonds by how they are secured. Here we have such bond types as mortgage bonds, debentures and notes.

Bonds may be further divided into types by the rights and privileges which are attached to them, such as those of redemption, conversion and sinking fund. Thus, we have redeemable bonds, sinking fund and purchase fund bonds, income bonds, extendible and retractable bonds, serial bonds and convertible bonds, to name a few.

Through various combinations of provisions for security and special features, a considerable number of different types of bonds have been brought into existence. The characteristics of any given bond can be determined by examining its title.

Let's start off by looking at the types of security behind a bond.

Security

Generally speaking, a bond is a debt instrument with a pledge of an asset behind it. If the issuer can't pay the interest or return the principal at maturity, the lenders have a claim on that asset. A debenture, on the other hand, is a debt issue without a physical asset pledged as collateral.

Then what's the physical asset behind Government of Canada bonds?

All those executive jets they use to get to conferences in Hawaii!

Well, just to make things a little more confusing, the term *bonds* is often used to refer to any debt issue, regardless of its security. Government of Canada bonds really aren't bonds, because there is no asset behind them. They're debentures, but we use the broader term *bonds* to refer to them. Keep in mind, though, that the government's powers of taxation can function as a type of security for its debt issues.

Mortgage Bonds

Those of you who own houses know that a mortgage is a legal document containing an agreement to pledge land, buildings, or equipment as security for a loan. It entitles the lender to take over ownership of these properties if you fail to pay interest or repay principal when due. The mortgage is held by the lender until the loan is repaid and is then cancelled or destroyed. It is not exercised unless you fail to satisfy the terms of the loan.

There is no fundamental difference between a mortgage and a mortgage bond except in form. Both are issued to secure property to the lender in the event of failure to repay a loan.

Since it is impractical for a corporation to issue separate mortgages securing portions of its properties to each lender, the same result is achieved by issuing one mortgage on its properties. The mortgage is then deposited with a trustee, usually a trust company, which acts for all lenders or investors in safeguarding their interests under the terms of the loan contract described in the mortgage. The amount of the loan is divided into convenient portions, usually $1,000, or multiples of $1,000, and each investor receives a bond as evidence of his proportionate participation in the loan to the company and the claim under the terms of the mortgage. This instrument is a mortgage bond.

First Mortgage Bonds

First mortgage bonds are the senior securities of a company because they constitute a first charge on the company's assets, earnings and undertakings before unsecured current liabilities are paid. Study each first mortgage issue to ascertain exactly what properties are covered by the mortgage. Most Canadian first mortgage bonds carry a first and specific charge against the company's fixed assets and a *floating charge* on all other assets. They are generally regarded as the best security a company can issue, particularly if the mortgage applies to all fixed assets of the company owned now and those acquired later. This last phrase is called the *after acquired clause.*

Collateral Trust Bonds

A collateral trust bond is one which is secured, not by a pledge of property as in a mortgage bond, but by physical pledge of other securities.

In order to provide a greater measure of security for a mortgage bond, collateral in the form of bonds and stocks may also be pledged. Such bonds are called *mortgage and collateral trust bonds*. First Mortgage and Collateral Trust bonds are secured by first mortgage and by the deposit with the trustee of other corporate securities such as bonds or shares of subsidiaries.

Debentures

A debenture in simple terms is an unsecured bond. It is a direct obligation, or a promise to pay, of the issuing company, but it does not have a specific claim or assignment on assets or property. A debenture ranks behind current liabilities, if so specified, and/or first and general mortgage bonds. In effect, the security is the general credit of the issuer. Sometimes, they are partly secured by certain assets which are not sufficient to provide a full mortgage, such as the assets of a subsidiary or a regional operation. In such cases they are known as *secured debentures.*

Corporate Debentures

Debentures are issued by corporations for several reasons. One is that the nature of the business may be commercial or mercantile and there are few assets which can be pledged under a mortgage. Another that the fixed assets have already been pledged under a closed mortgage which does not permit the issuance of further bonds. Some corporations are also so well established and so highly regarded that they can borrow from investors on favourable terms without having to pledge any company assets. Or, sometimes it's not possible to establish clear title to some land and buildings.

Subordinated Debentures

Subordinated debentures are debentures which are junior to another security issued by the company or another debt assumed by the company.

Corporate Notes

A corporate note is simply an unsecured promise made by the borrower to pay interest and repay the funds borrowed at a specific date or dates. Corporate notes rank behind all other fixed interest securities of the borrower.

Finance companies frequently use a type of note called a *secured note* or a *collateral trust note*. When you buy a car on credit, you make a cash down payment and sign a series of notes agreeing to make additional payments on specified dates. The automobile dealer takes these notes to a finance company which discounts them and pays the dealer in cash. Finance companies pledge notes like these as security for collateral trust notes. These notes are of various maturities and are sold to individual investors with substantial portfolios as well as to financial institutions.

Debt Classified by Features

Now let's look at some of the features that a bond could have. We've already talked about extendibles and retractables, but there are others.

Redeemable (or Callable) Bonds and Debentures

Corporate bond or debenture issues usually have a call feature that may be used at the corporation's option. The call price is usually set above the par value of the bond to compensate the holder for the loss of coupon income that will result from the redemption. The closer the bond is to its maturity date before it is redeemed, the less is the hardship to the investor. The redemption price is therefore often on a graduated scale and the premium payment becomes less as the bond draws closer to maturity. Debt which cannot be called prior to maturity is known as non-callable or non-redeemable.

Sinking Fund and Purchase Fund Bonds and Debentures

Sinking funds are sums of money which are set aside out of earnings each year to provide for the repayment of all or part of a debt issue by maturity. Most corporate debt issues carry a sinking fund provision, which is as binding on the issuer as any mortgage provision. A debt issue which carries a sinking fund arrangement usually indicates this in its title.

The sinking fund is a convenience to the issuer as some of the issue is paid off earlier than the maturity date, thus lessening the cash drain when eventual maturity is reached. It is not really a convenience for the holder since it may result in your bonds being called, even though you may have been planning to hold them till maturity.

Some companies prefer a purchase fund over a sinking fund. A fund is set up to retire through purchases in the market a specified amount of the outstanding bonds or debentures if purchases can be made at or below a stipulated price.

The purchase fund normally retires less of an issue than a sinking fund, there are no provisions for calling bonds as in the case of a sinking fund, and there are normally fewer mandatory features.

Occasionally, a company will have a sinking fund and a purchase fund together.

Convertible Bonds and Debentures

Convertible debentures combine certain advantages of a bond with the option of exchanging the bond for common shares. In effect, a convertible bond gives you a play on the common shares of the company.

Convertible debentures or bonds possess a special right to be exchanged into common shares on specifically determined terms called the *conversion privilege*. They possess the characteristics of bonds and debentures inasmuch as they carry a fixed interest rate and a definite maturity date. They offer possibilities of capital appreciation through the right to convert them into common shares at stated prices over stated periods.

Why Convertible Debentures are Issued

The addition of a conversion privilege makes a debenture more saleable. It tends to lower the cost of the money borrowed and may enable the company to raise equity capital indirectly on terms more favourable than through the sale of common shares.

The convertible has also been used to interest investors in providing capital for companies when they would not have been interested in buying relatively low-yielding or non-dividend paying common shares.

The convertible debenture is a two-way security – one which combines much of the safety and certainty of income of the bond with the option to convert into common shares with their prospects of increasing in value. The convertible has a special appeal for the investor who wants to share in the company's growth but wishes to avoid any substantial risk and is willing to accept the lower yield of the convertible in order to profit from growth in the common shares.

Characteristics of Convertible Debentures

In most convertible debentures, the conversion price is graduated upward over the years to encourage early conversion. In view of the ability of most Canadian companies to grow in net worth and earning capacity, this arrangement would seem to be reasonable.

Convertible debentures may normally be converted into stock at any time up until the conversion privilege expires. They are normally callable – usually at a small premium and after reasonable notice.

A Forced Conversion Clause

This clause is built into certain convertible debt issues to give the issuing company more scope in calling in the debt for redemption under certain circumstances. Such a redemption provision usually states that once the market price of the common stock exceeds a specified level for a specific number of days, the company can call the bonds for redemption at a stipulated price. The price, of course, would be much lower than the level at which the convertible debt would be trading due to the rise in the price of the common stock. Holders would choose to convert rather than have their debt called away at the lower redemption price.

This provision is an advantage to the issuing company rather than to the debt holder. The forced conversion can improve the company's debt-equity ratio and enable new debt financing to take place. However, it is not onerous to the debt holder to the point of detracting from an issue when it is first sold.

How do we know which convertible to choose?

Choosing Convertible Debentures

Here are some rules to follow when choosing a convertible for purchase:

- try to get as high a quality debenture as you can;
- buy it as close as possible to the price it would be worth if it had no conversion privilege;
- look for a conversion privilege which is realistic in terms of your estimate of the company's future growth;
- buy the convertible when stock prices are depressed, if the convertible is at a discount. There is no point in buying a convertible if

the conversion prices are above not only the present price but the prices at which you estimate the shares will sell in the years covered by the privilege.

Market Performance of Convertibles

Market prices of convertible debentures are influenced by their investment value and by the price level of the underlying common shares. In general, their prices rise along with increases in the prices of the common shares, and decline in value when the common stock price falls, but only to the levels at which they represent competitive values as straight debenture investments.

Convertible debentures tend to behave as follows. When the stock of the issuing company is well below the conversion price, the convertible debenture acts like a straight debenture, responding to the general level of interest rates, the activity of the sinking fund and the quality of the security.

When the stock approaches the conversion price, a *premium* appears. For example, a $1,000 debenture is convertible into 40 shares of stock ($25 per share). This convertible will sell somewhat above $1,000, perhaps at $1,100. This premium reflects the desires of investors to hold a two-way security. Although what constitutes a reasonable premium varies, 15% to 20% or lower is frequently considered attractive.

$$\text{Conversion Cost Premium} = \frac{\text{cost of debenture - cost of stock}}{\text{cost of stock}} \ X \ 100$$

When the common stock rises above the conversion price, the debenture will rise in price accordingly and is then said to be *selling off the stock*. If in our example the common stock rises to $30 per share, how will that affect the price of the convertible debenture?

It will rise to 40 times $30, or $1,200, plus some premium.

Pay-back Period

That's right. *The pay-back period* on a convertible debenture is an important evaluation tool for these securities. Pay-back period is the time it takes the convertible to recoup its premium through its higher yield, compared with the dividend that is paid on the stock. Pay-back periods of two years or less are usually considered attractive.

$$Pay\text{-}back\ period\quad =\quad \frac{conversion\ cost\ premium}{debenture\ yield\ -\ stock\ yield}$$

Floating Rate Debentures

Floating rate debentures have proved popular because of the protection they offer to investors during periods of very volatile interest rates. When interest rates are moving up, the interest paid is adjusted up-ward, with a resultant beneficial effect on the price and yield of the debentures. The disadvantage to these debentures is evident when their interest payable moves down as a result of a drop in rates. The mini-mum rate on the debentures can provide some protection to this proc-ess, though it is normally relatively low.

I've heard people talking about money market bonds. Why haven't you?

The Money Market

Sorry, Jason. A company wanting to borrow for a short term will do so on what is called the money market. This refers to the market for short-term credit instruments such as treasury bills, non-financial commercial paper, negotiable bank paper, finance company paper and the like. Maturities may be up to one year but usually are 90 days or less and sometimes only one day. This market brings those with temporarily idle funds together with short-term borrowers.

It allows quick, convenient low cost trading in almost any volume. At the centre of the money market are investment dealers, especially those designated as *money market dealers.* Most of the activity occurs in Toronto and Montreal and is conducted by telephone by these dealers, making the market easily accessible to all parts of the country as well as to foreign financial centres.

Who is involved in this market? I'm certainly not.

Participants in the money market essentially are those who enter the market to raise short-term funds or to invest cash surpluses. Funds may be raised by selling holdings of money market instruments, by borrowing from financial institutions (usually chartered banks) or by issuing new short-term debt instruments. Such borrowers must have high and accepted credit standings. Suppliers of funds in the money market are those who buy money market instruments or make short-term loans, that is, those whose cash requirements are some time in the future and can earn some interest income by holding interest-bearing liquid assets instead of non-earning cash. Participants include all levels of government, chartered banks and other financial institutions, finance companies, non-financial corporations and individuals.

The money market provides both users and suppliers of capital a choice of how they borrow or invest. Users may borrow from their bankers or they may issue money market securities. Suppliers, on the other hand, may deposit their cash with their banker or acquire securities. Greater flexibility enables participants to proceed in the way more advantageous to them. Market interest rates often enable borrowers using the money market to borrow for less than from the banks. Higher rates of return frequently may be earned from money market instruments than by depositing funds in bank accounts. The choices available to users and suppliers of capital has created a highly competitive and efficient money market.

Yes, but what exactly gets traded by all these people and companies?

Most money market instruments have some common characteristics. Denominations are usually in $100,000 multiples, but some notes are available in amounts as low as $1,000. Most paper has a stated maturity, but the term of corporate paper can be negotiated and some may be cashed in advance of maturity, although it usually provides a lower return if cashed. Because of their short-term nature, these securities do not usually pay interest as such – instead, you buy them for less then their maturity value and hold them until they mature at par. Let's say you have $10,000 to invest. You might see a money market security with a maturity of three months trading at 98. The maturity value is 100, so you could spend $9,800 and buy $10,000 of that security. Now you just have to wait three months until it matures at 100, or $10,000. You've made $200 on your $9,800 investment, and you've done it in 90 days, or one quarter of a year. Your return or yield would be 2.04% in 90 days; on an annualized basis it would be about 8.16%.

Here is a brief description of the major money market instruments:

Government of Canada Treasury Bills

Treasury bills are the focal point of the money market. They are virtually risk-free and thus acceptable to all lenders. They are very liquid, and large volumes can be bought and sold quickly without significant yield change. New bills are auctioned every week. Accordingly, it is quite simple to acquire outstanding bills or to bid for new issues with approximately the desired term. T-bills, as they are known, are issued with terms of 91, 182 and 364 days.

Government of Canada Bonds (due in three years or less)

The government could have issued a bond eight years ago that would mature in ten years, so now it would only have two years left until maturity. This type of bond would also trade on the money market, even though it wasn't created as a money market instrument.

The quality of these bonds is the same as that of treasury bills, but liquidity generally tends to be somewhat lower.

Provincial and Municipal Short-term Paper

Provinces issue paper on their own authority and can authorize their wholly-owned Crown corporations to issue short-term instruments. Municipal governments also borrow under their own authority. Credit ratings vary and liquidity is usually somewhat limited. At one time or another all the provinces have issued treasury bills, as have many of their Crown corporations, but only the largest municipalities have entered this market.

Finance Company (or Acceptance) Paper

Finance companies were the first to issue paper and become regular short-term borrowers in the market. In some cases, the paper is secured by specific assets such as instalment obligations of the companies' customers; in other cases, the backing is the general credit of the issuer. Paper usually is issued through investment dealers. Terms are often negotiable.

Commercial Paper (Non-financial Corporations)

Here is where your average corporation borrows money on a short-term basis. Commercial paper is not specifically secured but is usually supported by stand-by lines of credit at the issuers' bankers. In some cases (which also apply to finance companies) there is a parent company guarantee. As in the case of finance company paper, commercial paper is issued in interest-bearing or discount form with terms of a few days to a year. It is usually placed through investment dealers who may act as principals or as agents. Some paper may also be placed directly with lenders by the non-financial borrower.

Bankers' Acceptances

A bankers' acceptance is a commercial draft, or a written instruction to make payment, issued by a non-financial corporation that has been accepted by the borrower's bank. *Accepted* here means that the payment of interest and principal is guaranteed by the borrower's bank. Bankers consider acceptances carrying their mark to be liabilities of the bank, but the issuer must make funds available to the bank on the maturity date. The market yield on acceptances is usually a little lower than on commercial paper because they are backed by the credit of the issuer as well as by its bank, but the accepting fee charged by the banks makes the cost of borrowing the money a little higher. Paper is usually issued on a discount basis through money market dealers who may act as agents or principals.

Chartered Bank Paper

Canadian chartered banks issue a wide variety of deposit instruments designed to attract deposits from those with cash to invest. Most of them are modifications of pass book deposits. Bearer deposit notes or bearer term notes are types of bank paper traded in the money market. They are transferable and are sold and traded on a discount basis. In most cases, these notes are issued by banks directly to their customers.

Non-Transferable Vehicles

In addition to the marketable instruments just described, there are non-transferable vehicles for investment which usually are registered in the investor's name and carry a specific rate of return for a specific term. Some are redeemable prior to maturity with an interest rate reduction. The largest of these are trust company Guaranteed Investment Certificates – GICs, and chartered bank Certificates of Deposit – CDs.

The chartered banks also offer swapped deposits. Such a transaction consists of a spot purchase of foreign currency, usually U.S. dollars, with the proceeds deposited at the bank for a specified period and bearing an appropriate rate of interest. At the time of the spot purchase, a forward sale is made in the same account for a future date identical to the maturity date of the deposit and, thus, the investor has a fully hedged foreign currency deposit. The rate of return is the rate on the deposit, plus or minus the spread on the exchange swap.

You can see that the money market operates in a highly flexible way to maximize the use of available but temporarily idle funds. It serves a broad spectrum of borrowers and lenders, and new instruments and techniques are constantly being developed. It has grown greatly in size and sophistication in a comparatively short period of time.

I've heard that bond traders can make a lot of money buying and selling bonds. They can't be doing it in the money market, since prices there aren't going to fluctuate much if the maturity value is only a month or two away.

It's true that short-term bonds won't fluctuate in price as much as long-term bonds, although when you're trading millions of dollars of money market instruments it doesn't take much of a price change to realize a decent profit.

When people think about the securities markets, they tend to concentrate on the stock market alone. Tonight I've tried to show you that the bond market is also worthy of your attention. And learning about the forces that drive it can increase your understanding of the equity markets. We'll focus on equities next week. See you then.

Summary

Borrowed money is one of the two major components of a company's capital structure. Much of this money is acquired through the issuance of bonds and debentures. These debt issues have certain characteristics such as semi-annual interest payments, a maturity date, a redemption feature, and denomination size. Once issued, bonds trade on an over-the-counter secondary market. This market is regulated by the IDA and investment dealers are important participants in it.

Bond interest is taxed at the holder's regular tax rate. 75% of any capital gains that arise from selling a bond are taxable at the seller's regular rate.

A bond is a series of promises to pay specified amounts of money at specified times. How much are all of those promises worth today? To find out, we must determine the present value of each payment, be it a coupon or the principal, given today's interest rates. The bond will be worth the sum of the present value of all these payments. We can then compare this value to the bond's market price to see if a buying opportunity exists. Zero coupon bonds are also priced exactly this way, except there is only one payment to deal with. Zeros have some characteristics that make them different than regular bonds. They don't pay interest, there are differing tax considerations, they are more volatile than regular bonds, and their compounding aspect eliminates reinvestment risk.

Bonds prices fluctuate along with interest rates. Since a bond's coupon payment is fixed, it is the price that must change to bring the bond's yield into line with current rates. Other factors that affect bond prices are the issuer's credit rating, the term, the coupon rate and whether the bond has any special features. Investors can use bond switching to take advantage of price fluctuations.

There are a number of ways to classify bonds. One way is by the security behind the issue: from a first mortgage bond to a subordinated debenture. Another is by the bond's features: extendible, retractable, sinking or purchase fund, or convertible. A conversion feature probably has the largest affect on a bond's value, as it links the bond to the price movements of the company's common shares. Conversion cost premium and payback period formulae can help to evaluate a convertible's worth.

The money market is the part of the bond market where short-term debt is traded. Treasury bills are the most important money market instrument, but there are a variety of other government and corporate issues that trade there.

Chapter 4
Stocks

Features of common and preferred shares and how to choose them.

Last week we talked about investing in a company by loaning it money, through such instruments as bonds and debentures. There is, however, a more fundamental way of investing in a company, and that's by purchasing its stock – by becoming one of the owners of the company.

Investing in a company's "equity capital" can be a rewarding way to participate in a company's success, but it can also be much riskier. If the company performs well, the value of its stock could skyrocket – every investor's dream – and you'll reap a small fortune. But if it fails, the value of the stock could tumble to pennies, or to nothing.

Always remember that a company must pay off its debts – including bank loans and interest owed on bonds and debentures – before its owners see a cent in dividends. And if it fails and has to be liquidated, the creditors have first claim on the assets. As a shareholder, you're entitled to whatever is left. Possibly nothing.

With this caution ringing in your ears, let's talk about the advantages of buying stock. The first part of our discussion will focus on common shares; later we'll talk about preferred shares, rights and warrants.

Common Shares

Ownership of the common stock of a company is usually – but not always – accompanied by the right to a say in the way the company is run. This includes the right to attend the annual meeting, to elect the directors who guide and control the business operations, and to vote on special questions, such as the sale, merger or liquidation of the business or the amendment of the charter.

Voting Rights

To vote, you must have shares issued in your own name or be in possession of a completed proxy form. Usually, each common shareholder has one vote for each share owned. Shareholders often sign proxy forms giving company management their vote. Even so, an annual meeting is a valuable opportunity to question management and make your views known. And there is always the possibility of the high drama of a "proxy fight", with management and challengers campaigning for proxy support before or during a meeting.

If the company issues 100,000 shares and you buy 5,000 of them, then you own 5% of the company. This entitles you to 5,000 votes, or a total of 5% of all votes.

Potential for Capital Appreciation

When a company "goes public", its stock becomes available to the public, normally through a listing on a stock exchange, or by trading in an OTC market. Investors are free to buy and sell the company's shares; depending on its performance and prospects, the market value of the stock can rise or fall, possibly many times. If you "buy low, sell high" – always the preferred scenario – you profit from your investment with a capital gain when you sell.

A stock's price can rise substantially over time. Most companies believe it is good corporate strategy to keep the market price of their shares in a popular price range, say $10-$20. Past that point companies will consider a stock split or subdivision to bring the price back into the preferred range.

Stock is usually sold in board lots of 100, and blocks costing more than $1,000 or $2,000 are considered too rich for many investors' blood.

The mechanics of a stock split are straight-forward. First, the company's directors pass and submit a by-law for approval by a vote of the voting common shareholders at a special meeting. Depending on the current market price of the shares, the split could be on any basis such as two new shares for one old share; or three new for one old; or even ten for one.

When a split becomes effective, the market price of the new shares reflects the basis of the split.

In a four-for-one split, the market price of shares selling at $100 (pre-split basis) will sell somewhere in the $25 range after the split.

When a split is first announced, the initial effect on the market price of the stock may be bullish. There can be a modest surge in the price of the shares on increased volume. Dividend increases, often announced at the same time, contribute to the initial bullish impact. The effect of a split on the share's market price after the initial flurry depends on several important factors, such as the company's earnings trend and the current stage of the stock market cycle.

Alternately, a company may implement a *reverse stock split* or *consolidation*, reducing each shareholder's total shareholdings in a company. Reverse splits occur most frequently among low-priced junior mining and oil exploration companies.

In a 1 for 4 reverse split, a shareholder owning 100 shares of stock would own only 25 new shares after the split. If the shares were selling at $0.25 before the split, the new shares would probably trade near $1.00 per share.

A reverse split raises the market price of the new shares and can put the company in a better position to raise new exploration capital.

Marketability

To make (or lose) money when selling stock, you have to find someone willing to buy it from you. That's usually not a hard thing to accomplish; you can find a buyer for most Canadian securities (in reasonable quantities) within a day or so – if you can agree on a price. It's a relatively simple matter with few legal formalities.

So what do you do, stand on a street corner with a sign?

The Stock Exchanges

Not quite, Jason. The vast majority of sales are accomplished through the facilities of stock exchanges. There are about 200 exchanges in over 60 nations around the world, including the five in Canada: the Montreal Exchange, the Toronto Stock Exchange, the Vancouver Stock Exchange, the Alberta Stock Exchange in Calgary and the Winnipeg Stock Exchange.

During trading hours, Canada's exchanges receive thousands of buy and sell orders from all parts of the country and abroad. The process begins when you place an order with your Investment Advisor to sell or buy shares. If the proposed price is acceptable, the order is usually quickly matched by someone else's buy or sell order, delivered through their IA, and the transaction is completed. Each IA receives a commission from their client for putting through the trade.

The Over-the-Counter Market

There is also trading through the Over-the-Counter (OTC) Market, also known as the unlisted market. Although complete statistics aren't available, the volume of unlisted equity business in Canada is smaller than the volume of stock exchange transactions. Many junior issues trade OTC on the Canadian Dealing Network (CDN), but so too do the shares of a few conservative industrial companies whose boards of directors have for one reason or another decided not to seek stock exchange listing for one or more issues of their equities.

Over-the-counter trading in equities is conducted in a similar manner to bond trading. One veteran described the OTC market as a "market without a marketplace", a way of buying and selling securities by negotiation as well as by auction, which is the method used on stock exchanges. A network of telephones and computer equipment effectively links hundreds of brokers and investment dealers all over the country. Transactions over this network are carried out by traders who specialize in OTC securities. Trading goes on for longer than stock exchange hours, and in a busy market can take up an entire business day.

 If I buy shares on any of these markets, aren't I buying them from another investor who is selling them? How does the company benefit from my buying their shares?

When a company first sells its shares to investors, the proceeds from the sale go to the company. After that, Pat, you're right: when these outstanding shares are subsequently sold by their holders, the selling price is paid to the seller of the shares and not to the corporation. Shares, therefore, may be transferred from one owner to another without affecting the operations of the company or its finances. But companies do keep a close eye on their share price. Even though they don't profit directly if the price goes up, should they want to issue more shares down the road, it will be at more or less the then current market price. So a higher price down the road will benefit them when it comes time to sell new shares.

Companies may also purchase some or all of their own common shares either by tender or on the open market for cancellation, subsequent resale, or for use in dividend reinvestment plans. This practice is popularly known as a *buy-back.*

Constraints

In some circumstances, there may be constraints on the marketability of shares. Stock exchanges and securities commissions have the power to halt or suspend trading in a company's shares pending a major development, an important announcement or an investigation of a company's affairs. In some cases, the sale of shares of certain companies to persons who are not Canadian citizens or not residents of Canada is restricted. These companies, known as *constrained share companies,* include banks, trust and insurance companies, broadcasting and communications companies.

 So owing common shares gives me a vote and the potential for capital appreciation. What else can I expect?

The Right to Receive Dividends

If a company performs well, you may have the happy experience of seeing it post a profit. If it's a fast-growing business, or in a period of expansion, its directors may decide to plough the profits back into the business. A more mature company, however, will likely share some or all the good fortune with it owners, through the declaration of dividends.

Unlike interest on debt, dividends on common shares are not a contractual obligation. The board of directors decides whether to pay a dividend, the amount and payment date. An announcement is made in advance of the payment date. Companies may pay dividends quarterly, semi-annually or annually.

Some companies paying common share dividends designate a specified amount that will be paid each year as a regular dividend. The term *regular* indicates to investors that payments will be maintained barring a major collapse in earnings.

Some major companies give their preferred and common shareholders the option of participating in an automatic *Dividend Reinvestment Plan.* In such a plan, the company diverts the shareholders' dividends to the purchase of additional shares of the company. The result is a kind of automatic savings plan, which solves the problem of reinvesting small amounts of cash. Participating shareholders acquire a gradually increasing share position in the company, and, because purchases by the plan are made regularly, the advantages of *dollar cost averaging* are obtained.

Dollar cost averaging: investing a fixed amount of money in the same security at regular intervals, resulting in a reduced average cost per share.

Unfortunately, reinvested dividends are taxable to the shareholder as ordinary cash dividends even though the dividends are not received as cash.

Favourable Tax Treatment of Dividends and Capital Gains

The tax system in Canada provides several benefits to investors in common shares, including:

- the federal dividend tax credit, which makes the purchase of dividend-paying shares of taxable Canadian companies relatively attractive for persons in lower tax brackets;

- stock savings plans, which entitle residents of several provinces to deduct up to a set amount from the cost of certain stocks purchased in their province.

Preferred Shares

Preferred shares are a hybrid investment offering the best – and the worst – of both the equity and debt worlds.

Preferred shareholders, like common shareholders, are part owners of the company whose stock they hold – but they normally have no vote in company affairs. Like debt instruments such as bonds and debentures, preferreds are fixed income securities, offering a fixed dividend out of net earnings. Since they don't benefit directly from a company's increased profits, they don't offer the same potential for capital gain as do common shares, and their price doesn't normally fluctuate on the market as much as the common stock might.

However, unlike debt interest, dividends are not a legal requirement. Dividends are paid from current or past earnings. If the directors decide to omit the payment of a preferred dividend – perhaps to preserve working capital in an emergency – there is very little the preferred shareholders can do about it. Normally, however, no dividends are paid to common shareholders until preferred shareholders have received full payment of dividends to which they are entitled.

Thus, the preferred shareholder occupies a position between that of the common shareholder and that of the company's creditors. If the company's ability to pay interest and dividends deteriorates because of lower earnings, the preferred shareholder is better protected than the common shareholders but junior to the claims of the debtholders.

Similarly, if the company is wound up or dissolved, preferred shareholders line up behind the creditors and debtholders. At the end of the line is the common shareholder, who has to be content with anything that is left after all creditor, debtholder and preferred shareholder claims have been met.

How does a company decide whether to issue preferreds, common, or debt?

Issuing Preferred Shares

Since the greatest similarities are between preferreds and debt, that's probably where the choice would lie. There are a number of factors the company would consider. Companies normally find issuing preferred shares a more expensive way to raise capital, compared to bonds or debentures. Interest on debt instruments, you see, is a tax-deductible expense, because interest is considered a legitimate cost of doing business. Dividends, however, because they are a distribution of company profits, are not tax-deductible and are paid with more costly after-tax dollars.

Nonetheless, circumstances sometimes do justify a new preferred share issue.

And what might these be?

First, from the company's viewpoint, straight preferreds do not create the demands that a debt issue creates. With preferreds there is no maturity date which may come at a financially awkward time. If the company's directors need to omit a preferred dividend, they can do so without jeopardizing the company's solvency. If interest isn't paid when due on debt issues, the bond or debenture holders have recourse to seizing assets. This isn't an option open to preferred shareholders denied their dividend.

Also, there are times when it simply isn't feasible to market a new debt issue. Perhaps the market is temporarily unreceptive to new debt issues. The company may already have a lot of debt outstanding, and preferreds are issued to add balance to the capital structure and to increase the equity base. Or the company's existing assets may be heavily mortgaged already; or it may operate in a business which has few assets available for pledging, like a sales finance company. Finally, a company may have a low apparent tax rate, which means less of a burden to pay dividends from after-tax profits.

Second, when a company has decided it will not or cannot issue bonds or debentures, it may find conditions unfavourable for selling common shares. The stock market may be falling or inactive, or business prospects may be uncertain. However, in such circumstances preferred shares might be marketed as a compromise acceptable to both the issuing company and investors. Straight preferreds also offer the advantage of avoiding the dilution of equity that results from a new issue of common shares.

Who buys preferred shares?

Conservative investors seeking income purchase preferred shares, in part to take advantage of the Dividend Tax Credit. The system of taxation for dividends results in less tax being paid on dividend income than on an equivalent amount of interest income. The tax system recognizes that since dividends are paid out of company profits, they have already been taxed before being paid to shareholders.

Preferred shares are also purchased as an income investment by Canadian companies, because dividends paid by one resident taxable

Canadian company to a similar company are not taxable in the hands of the receiving company. This is not the case with debt interest. When Canadian Company One purchases a debt issue of Canadian Company Two, the interest received by Company One is fully taxable in Company One's hands.

Dividend Tax Credit

Assume an investor in a 26% federal tax bracket receives $1,000 in dividends.

1. Gross up dividend by 25% $1,000 + 250 + 1,250

2. Calculate federal tax   26% of 1,250 = 325

3. Calculate dividend tax credit   13.33% of 1,250 = 167

4. Calculate federal tax payable 325 - 167 = $158

Like common shares, preferreds can be listed on a stock exchange or traded over-the-counter.

Preferred Features

The description of the rights of a preferred shareholder are found in the charter of the company. A company wishing to issue preferred shares must apply to make the necessary changes to its charter, unless the existing charter provides for issuance of preferred shares at the discretion of the directors.

I will describe some features that could be built into all types of preferred shares. Some features strengthen the issuer's position; others protect the purchaser's position. The final selection represents a compromise in that the new issue will offer safeguards to the buyer without unduly restricting the issuer.

If you want to get more information on the features of a particular preferred share, your IA should be able to help. You can also do your own research through the Financial Post Historical Report for that company, or special annual "Survey" books such as the Financial Post Survey of Industrials.

Cumulative and Non-cumulative

Most Canadian preferred shares have a *cumulative feature* built into their terms. If a company's financial condition weakens because of a decline in earnings, the directors may reluctantly decide to omit a preferred dividend. The unpaid dividends accumulate or pile up in what is known as *arrears.*

I've made some dumb investments over the years, but why would anyone buy a preferred that wasn't paying its dividend?

Most people wouldn't, and a decision not to pay a dividend will cause the market price of the preferred shares to decline as investors flee the stock. The shares assume a speculative aspect which will become more pronounced if subsequent dividends are passed, and arrears continue to accumulate. Later, if the company's earnings improve or if losses change to profit, some investors may buy the preferred on speculation that dividends will resume. And don't forget that all arrears of cumulative preferred dividends must be paid before common dividends are paid or before the preferred shares are redeemed. If a partial or complete repayment of arrears materializes, payment is made to the preferred shareholders owning stock at time of repayment. Imagine you had bought a preferred at $7.50 with $2.50 of dividend arrears. If payments resume, you've made a 33% return, and the price of the preferred will also increase. No payments are made to preferred shareholders who previously sold their stock and no interest is paid on arrears.

Few Canadian preferred shares are non-cumulative, where the shareholder is entitled to payment of a specified dividend in any year only when declared. When a non-cumulative preferred dividend is passed, arrears do not accrue and the preferred shareholder is not entitled to "catch-up" payments if dividends resume. For this reason the dividend position of non-cumulative preferred shares is very weak.

Callable and Non-callable

Issuers of preferred shares frequently reserve the right to *call* or redeem preferred issues. A call feature is a convenience to the issuer, not normally an advantage to the purchaser.

As with callable corporate debt, callable preferreds usually provide for payment of a small premium above the amount of per share asset entitlement fixed by the charter, as compensation to the investor whose shares are being called in. Accepted practice is for the issuer to give 30 days' notice of intention to redeem.

It is usual to give the issuing company the privilege of buying shares for cancellation on the open market or through invitations for tenders addressed to all holders. The price paid under these circumstances generally must not exceed the par value of the preferred shares plus the premium provided for redemption by call.

Non-callable preferred shares cannot be called or redeemed. This feature is restrictive from the issuer's standpoint, in that it freezes a part of its capital structure for the life of the company. The feature nowadays is, therefore, rarely built into the terms of Canadian preferreds. It is advantageous to the purchaser since the investment cannot be redeemed.

Voting Privileges

Virtually all preferred shares are non-voting so long as preferred dividends are paid on schedule. However, once a stated number of preferred dividends have been omitted, it is common practice to assign voting privileges to the preferred.

Issuing companies may consider a non-voting feature advantageous, since it ensures the preferred shares have no say in running the company's affairs so long as dividend requirements are met.

However, preferred shareholders are usually given a vote on matters affecting the quality of their security – for example, increasing the amount of preferred stock authorized. Sometimes, preferred shareholder approval is obtained before a debt issue is created.

Purchase Funds and Sinking Funds

Many redeemable Canadian preferred shares have a *purchase fund* built into their terms. With this feature, the company agrees to retire, through purchases in the open market, a specified amount of preferred shares each year if stock is available at or below a stipulated price. However, if the purchase fund is not able to buy enough shares in the open market, no redemption is implemented.

A purchase fund is advantageous to preferred shareholders because it means that if the price of the shares declines in the market below a certain level, the fund will make every effort to buy specified amounts of shares for redemption. As a result, this type of issue has potential built-in market support.

Special Protective Provisions

Underwriters encourage companies creating new preferreds to build in specified protective provisions to safeguard the position of the preferred shareholder and make the issue more saleable. Here is a list of some of these provisions:

- restrictions on common dividends if they weaken the company's financial position;
- the right to vote if dividends are in arrears;
- restrictions on further preferred issues;
- restrictions on asset sales;
- restrictions on changing the terms of the preferred.

Is it only these protective provisions and the size of the dividend that separates one preferred from another?

Straight Preferreds

Actually there are also some special features that preferreds can have. To begin with, those with no special features are called straight preferreds. These are preferred shares with normal preferences as to asset and dividend entitlement ahead of the common shares. Straight preferreds may have any or all of the special features described earlier. Since straight preferreds pay a fixed rate of dividends, the shares trade in the market on a yield basis. As with the market price of bonds and debentures, if interest rates rise, the market price of straight preferreds will fall and if interest rates decline their price will rise.

$$Preferred \ = \ \frac{annual\ dividend}{share\ price}\ X\ \ 100$$

Special Types of Preferreds:

Convertible preferreds, on the other hand, are similar to convertible bonds and debentures because they enable you to convert the preferred into some other class of shares, usually common, at a predetermined price and for a stated period of time.

Conversion terms are set when the preferred is created and normally the conversion price is set at a modest premium, perhaps 10% - 15%

above the then prevailing market for the common. The purpose of the premium is to discourage an early conversion, which would defeat the purpose of the convertible offering. Virtually all conversion privileges expire after a stated period of time, usually five to twelve years from date of issue. Conversion terms may include conversion price changes at predetermined times.

If the common shares rise in price above the preferred's conversion price, the market price of the convertible preferred will rise accordingly. When this occurs, the preferred is described as *selling off the common stock* and the market action of the preferred will reflect the market action of the common. During this time the convertible preferred will usually sell at a premium above the price it might be expected to sell at, based on the conversion terms.

Once a convertible preferred is exercised it is not possible to convert back. No commission is charged on conversion and no capital gain or capital loss is incurred until the subsequent sale of shares received from conversion.

If the underlying common shares are split, the conversion terms are adjusted automatically on the basis of the larger number of new underlying shares.

Convertible Preferred Shares

- *provide a "two-way" security – the holder is in a more secure position than the common shareholder and yet can realize a capital gain if the market price of the common rises sufficiently*
- *usually provide a higher yield than the underlying common shares*
- *provide the right to obtain common shares through conversion without paying commission*
- *usually provide a lower yield than a comparable straight preferred*
- *are vulnerable to a decline in price if selling off the common and the price of the common declines*
- *sometimes convert into an odd number of common shares which may be more difficult to sell than a board lot*
- *revert to a straight preferred when the conversion period expires*

Why would a company issue a convertible preferred? Since the decision to convert is up to the investor, wouldn't the company lose control over the proportionate mix of common and preferred?

Convertible preferreds are issued either in markets where a straight preferred is difficult to sell or in a situation where a high level of dividend coverage is lacking. Because a conversion feature is popular with investors, the dividend can be less than that of a comparable straight preferred and the convertible preferred can still be saleable.

Forced Conversion

Acme Preferred:

price $35   conversion terms 1:1   common price $33   call price: $25

Acme calls the preferred shares.

Would you accept $25 or convert the preferreds into common?

Most convertible preferreds are redeemable, which gives the issuer the power to force a conversion into the underlying shares when the market price of the preferred rises above the redemption price. To force a conversion, management announces the redemption of the preferred at the call price as at a certain date. Convertible preferred shareholders convert their shares because of the price advantage. A forced conversion is implemented only if management decides there is an advantage to retiring the preferred by issuing new common shares.

Retractable Preferred Shares

- *provide a predetermined date(s) and price(s) to tender shares for retraction – the shorter the time interval to the retraction date, the less vulnerable is the stock's market price to increases in interest rates*

- *provide a capital gain if purchased at a discount from the retraction price and subsequently tendered at the retraction price*

- *will sell above the retraction price and at least as high as the redemption price if interest rates decline sufficiently*

- *do not retract automatically – if no action is taken by the holder during the election period(s), the retraction privilege will expire*

- *become straight preferred shares if not retracted when the election period expires*

Retractable Preferreds

While most preferred shares are redeemable, it is up to the issuer whether redemption actually occurs. As a retractable preferred shareholder, on the other hand, you can force the company to redeem the retractable preferred on a specified date and at a specified price. You can create a maturity date for the preferred by exercising the retraction privilege and tendering the shares to the issuer for redemption.

Variable or Floating Rate Preferreds

Identical in concept to variable or floating rate debentures, variable rate preferreds pay dividends in amounts that fluctuate to reflect changes in interest rates. If interest rates rise, so will dividend payments and vice versa.

Variable rate preferreds are issued during periods in the market when a straight preferred is hard to sell and the issuer has rejected making the issue convertible, because of potential dilution of common equity, or retractable, because holders could force redemption on a specified date. The issuer believes interest rates will not go much higher than they are now, but in any event is prepared to pay a higher dividend if interest rates rise. Of course, if interest rates decline, the issuer will pay a smaller dividend, subject in most cases to a guaranteed minimum rate.

Some preferred shares may have delayed variable rate features. Known as delayed floaters or fixed floaters, these shares entitle the holder to a fixed dividend for a predetermined period of time, after which the dividend becomes variable.

> ### Variable Rate Preferreds
>
> - *the dividend payout is tied to changes in interest rates on a predetermined basis*
>
> - *provide higher income if interest rates rise, but lower income if interest rates fall*
>
> - *provide a variable amount of annual income which is difficult to predict accurately but which will reflect prevailing interest rate levels*
>
> - *provide an investment with a market price less responsive to changes in interest rates vis-a-vis the market prices of straight preferred shares*
>
> ### Participating Preferred Shares
>
> - *provide the possibility of higher dividend income when the company's earnings permit*
>
> - *provide only a marginal advantage over the common shares if a limited participation feature is present*

Participating Preferreds

Participating preferred shares have certain rights to a share in the earnings of the company over and above their specified dividend rate.

Foreign-pay Preferreds

Most Canadian preferreds pay dividends in Canadian funds. However, it is possible for a company to create and issue preferreds with dividends and certain other features payable in or related to foreign funds. The key factor to selecting such a preferred is the desirability of receiving dividends in a currency other than Canadian funds. You benefit if the foreign currency rises against the Canadian dollar. If the foreign currency falls against the Canadian dollar, you will wish you had stuck to a straight preferred.

Rights and Warrants

Sometimes when a company wants to raise more money it will issue rights and/or warrants. These allow the shareholder to buy more shares directly from the company, usually at a price somewhat lower than the current market price of the old shares. This is a way for a company to raise additional funds in a way that favours existing shareholders.

The major difference between rights and warrants is their lifespan. Rights usually expire after a few weeks, while warrants can continue from one to several years. Both can trade on the market separately from the company's stock.

The customary method of making a rights offering is to issue one right for each common share outstanding. You can then combine the rights into the multiples required for one or more shares and subscribe. No commission is levied when you exercise the rights and acquire new shares. Normally fractional shares are not issued.

A ready market in the rights usually develops, permitting surplus rights to be sold or additional rights to be purchased. The possibility that the market price of the stock will fall below the subscription price is of major importance in setting the terms of a rights issue. If this happened, you wouldn't exercise your rights and the share issue will fail. To curb the risk of this occurring, many rights issues are underwritten by an investment dealer. In return for a fee, the underwriter will generally stand ready to purchase a certain number of the unsubscribed shares for at least the subscription price.

The value of a right closely resembles the difference between its subscription price and the market price of the stock. This amount is the right's intrinsic value. If the right is trading for more than its intrinsic value, we call the extra amount its time value. Once rights expire they are worthless and may not be exercised.

Intrinsic Value = stock price - subscription price

Time Value = right price - intrinsic value

Right Price = intrinsic value + time value

A warrant is often attached to new debt and preferred issues to make these issues more attractive to buyers, thereby functioning as a sweetener.

Like rights, warrants may have an intrinsic value and a time value. Intrinsic value is the amount by which the market price of the underlying common stock exceeds the exercise price of the warrant.

A warrant has no intrinsic value if the exercise price is above the current market value of the shares; however it will still usually have a market value known as time value because of perceived speculative potential up to the expiry date.

The main speculative attraction of warrants is their leverage potential. The price of a warrant is usually much less than the price of the underlying security and generally moves together with it. The capital appreciation of a warrant on a percentage basis can therefore greatly exceed that of the underlying security. This chart illustrates the concept of leverage. Assume there is a warrant with a market value of $4, exercisable at $12 on an underlying common stock whose market price is $15. If the common rises to $23 before the warrants expire, the warrants would rise to at least their intrinsic value of $11 (23 - 12), an increase of 175% of the original outlay. The common shares would have appreciated only 53%.

Of course, the reverse is true. A fall in the price of the common from $15 to $11 results in a 27% loss in share value compared with a potential 100% loss in the value of the warrant, assuming again that it has no time value.

Warrant exercisable at $12

	Stock at 15	Stock at 23	Stock at 11
Warrant Price	4	11	0
Intrinsic Value	3	11	0
Time Value	1	0	0
Stock $ Gain (Loss)		8	(4)
Stock % Gain (Loss)		53	(27)
Warrant $ Gain (Loss)		7	(4)
Warrant % Gain (Loss)		175	(100)

I know all about those 100% losses! Why don't we learn how to avoid them?

Good idea! Choosing the correct investment from among a wide variety of places to put your money is the most difficult job in investing. However, many people contemplating buying securities for the first time are too busy to obtain the necessary background and information to make these decisions on their own. To reduce avoidable mistakes, novice investors should seek the advice of a reputable securities firm or Investment Advisor before making an initial purchase of securities. While competent advice is important, it isn't an end in itself. The successful investor continually seeks more knowledge about the securities markets.

Gone are the days when an investor could rely on a stock tip overheard at a cocktail party! Information travels too fast these days, and that hot tip is most likely old news by now. Still, you shouldn't ignore all of your hunches when looking for a ripe stock. Let's say you hear that that discount electronics retailer up the street plans an initial public offering of stock. Last time you were in the store, it seemed to be doing a booming business. Maybe this company deserves a closer look as a possible investment.

Another source for investment tips is brokers' research reports. But unless you plan to put money into everything that has a "buy" recommendation attached to it, you'll have to be able to make sense of the report by knowing the language it uses.

Evaluating Stocks

What makes one stock worth buying over another? There are many different ways to judge a stock's merit. Strong profit performance is important. But this might already be reflected in the company's stock price, and the shares could already have run out of steam. Only a careful analysis will indicate whether a stock has further upside, based on forecasts for future earnings. This analysis, known as the price-to-earnings (or P/E) ratio, will be discussed in greater detail later.

Besides earnings, many analysts will focus on a company's balance sheet, where assets are matched against liabilities. By dividing the company's net asset value by the number of its shares outstanding, the analyst can learn whether the stock is undervalued or overvalued in the market relative to other companies that are in the same line of business.

Alternatively, a stock can be rated in the context of the economy. If interest rates are on a downswing, this would favour interest-sensitive stocks like banks and utilities. However, once an economic recovery takes hold and corporate earnings are heading higher, manufacturing and resource stocks should benefit.

Then there is simply the phenomenon of a hot stock. These Holy Grails of the stock market are so exceptional that they will outperform the market, regardless of the state of the economy or the particular industry. Finding these gems, however, requires a lot of skill, or luck, or both.

Still another way of evaluating stocks is known as technical analysis, which largely ignores the fundamental details of a company's sales and profits. Instead, the technical analyst may chart past trends in the movement of the company's stock price and in trading volumes in order to time the next significant move up or down in the shares. From these charts, the analyst expects to be able to spot heavy demand, indicating an uptrend in the stock, or sudden supply, suggesting a downtrend.

Here's an example of how technical analysis works. It is assumed that the news of a favourable development related to a company tends to spread from group to group in waves. First one group of people will buy the stock, and its price will go up on heavy volume. Then there will be a quiet period and the stock will sell off. After a while a new group of people will hear the news and buy the stock, and again it will go up on heavy volume. When the technical analyst spots this pattern on a chart, he is alerted to the buying, and probably will favour the stock.

So with all these different ways of evaluating a stock, which do I pay attention to?

Well, the answer is all of them, and none of them alone. Statistical analysis, such as the P/E ratio, or the net asset value per share, are helpful but must be used with caution. One ratio alone doesn't tell much. Ratios are not proofs, but clues to a judgment. Also, the significance of a ratio may vary between different types of companies in different industries. We'll talk more about financial ratios later.

Industry Types

As a first step in fundamental analysis, it is common practice to select industries which are likely to perform best during a given time period, say 12 to 24 months, and then to select individual companies that are likely to lead those industries. To identify the best companies for investment, we need to have a sense of how industries evolve, and what this means for stock prices. Broadly speaking, there are a few recognizable stages in an industry's evolution.

Emerging Industries

These develop new products or services to meet society's needs and demands. The transportation industry, for example, has gone from horses to cars to airplanes in a few decades. Similarly, rapid innovation is evident today in the electronics field, including personal computers and entertainment systems. Emerging industries might not always be directly accessible to equity investors: the companies might be privately owned, or the new technology might be just a small activity within a much larger company.

Growth Industries

These typically have sales and earnings that are consistently expanding at a faster rate than most industries. Such companies are called growth companies and their shares are growth stocks. Growth stocks generally have increased in value at well above average rates for at least five years, and are expected to continue to do so. A mere rise in price doesn't make a growth stock. Instead, the rise must be based on permanent factors, such as increasing earnings and value of assets.

Growth stocks usually have the following characteristics:

- a high rate of earnings on invested capital;
- retention and reinvestment of earnings, rather than paying much of this out in dividends;
- capable and aggressive management; and
- fertile opportunity for earnings growth.

Some current examples of growth industries include computer software and biotechnology.

Stable Industries

These have sales and earnings that are relatively stable and tend to hold up even in a recession. This stability, however, doesn't guarantee immunity from the downward momentum of a bear market, although price swings may be moderate. Such companies usually have the internal resources to weather difficult economic conditions successfully.

Companies in stable industries tend to fit into three main categories:

- Blue chip stocks are considered top investment quality companies that maintain earnings and dividends through good times and bad. They often show strong growth in sales and earnings, but are different from growth companies in that they are larger, have a certain market dominance and are more seasoned. Still, a blue chip stock offers no guarantee of continued performance, as company fortunes can and do change. Many investors consider Canada's major chartered banks to be blue chips.

- Defensive stocks are considered to be relatively immune to poor economic conditions. Utilities are an example in this category, because of the essential and continuing services they provide. Other industries in which sales hold up well even in economic downturns include brewing, pharmaceuticals and food wholesaling. However, other factors need to be considered when investing in these industries, such as price competition within the industry.

- Income stocks provide a generous dividend yield that is relatively well assured. At the same time, this attractive yield might imply a relatively low degree of price volatility and limited potential for capital appreciation. Shares of utility companies are also classified as income stocks, as well as blue chip and defensive stocks.

Be aware that not all stocks with high dividend yields are income stocks. For example, a high current yield may be the result of a large drop in the stock's price in anticipation of possible financial difficulties at the company.

Cyclical Industries

These includes companies with earnings that are particularly sensitive to the business cycle. Few, if any, industries are immune from the adverse effects of an overall business downturn, but the term cyclical applies to those where the effect on earnings is most pronounced. As business conditions improve, earnings tend to rebound dramatically. Examples of cyclical industries include steel, forest products, cement, automobiles, household appliances and heavy equipment.

Some companies are affected by seasonal factors, but this doesn't make them cyclical stocks. Brewing companies, for instance, have higher sales in the summer, but are relatively stable year to year.

Speculative Industries

These involve higher risk than normal equity investments, because of an absence of definitive information. Emerging industries, for instance, can be called speculative; there is no assurance that a particular company will be among the survivors that enjoy the benefit of a new technology. In Canada, speculative often refers to the so-called penny stocks, mainly junior mining and oil and gas ventures. The term speculative also is used when a growth company's stock is bid up sharply on an expectation of continuing exceptional growth. If these expectations suddenly deflate for some reason, the stock could plunge.

Declining Industries

These involve products for which demand is in decline due to changes in technology or consumer preference. However, companies in these situations can survive by diversifying operations or by acquiring other companies, if management takes appropriate action at an early stage. Steel manufacturing is an example of a declining industry. Many of the uses for steel have been supplanted by plastic compounds or other materials.

With industries broken down into those categories, shouldn't you invest in the emerging industries and growth stocks to get the biggest returns on investment?

For the investor with a high risk tolerance, yes. But for most people, a diversified portfolio of securities with a highly volatile stock balanced out by a stable defensive stock is preferable. Although this portfolio's overall return might be lower, there's less chance of losing the farm.

Evaluating stocks by industry also helps the analyst keep track of factors that affect all the companies in an industry. For example, swings in world commodity prices will affect most mining stocks, although some will be affected more than others. And most financial services companies are likely to feel the effects of a change in interest rates.

I usually hear about changes in interest rates. But how do I know when lumber prices are changing? Or, for that matter, when a company is coming out with a new product that might compete with another's existing product?

Reading the business section of a daily newspaper will help you catch some of this kind of information. Also, weekly or monthly business magazines usually have more in-depth articles on companies and the challenges they are facing. And investment newsletters usually try to provide the specific information that is critical to making an investment decision.

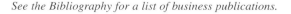

See the Bibliography for a list of business publications.

Although an informed investor wants to know when there is a change in the price of a commodity, such as lumber, it's probably too late at that point to buy those stocks. Cyclical stocks usually go up in anticipation of stronger commodity prices, not after the fact. So reading analysts' research reports, distributed by the various brokerage houses to their clients, could keep you informed of events that are expected to develop in the near future. Some of these forecasts are also reported in business newspapers.

Let's say I've decided I like the fundamentals of the steel industry, but wouldn't touch forestry stocks with a 10-foot pole. What do I do next?

Once you have identified an industry of interest, the next step is to look at the specific companies within that sector. This analysis should then lead to a comparative evaluation of all major companies in that industry. Each company will be unique in the way it does business and finances its operations.

Choosing a Company

Company analysis has two components: quantitative analysis, which draws heavily on data from published financial statements; and qualitative analysis, which attempts to assess intangible factors such as the quality of management. For both the professional analyst and the novice investor, a valuable source of information on a company is its annual report to shareholders, which usually can be obtained by phoning the company.

The average investor with little or no training in accounting usually finds it difficult to make sense of company financial statements. However, with just a little time invested, these statements are not hard to understand and interpret. They can reveal a great deal about a company's financial health.

Buying a company's shares amounts to an investment in its future prospects, which are difficult to forecast with accuracy. But the past often provides a clue to the future, and if you have some knowledge of a company's present financial position and its past earnings record, you are more likely to select securities that will stand the test of time. As we discussed, you will need to combine this information with an understanding of the industry in which the company operates, the economy in general, and the specific plans and prospects for the company in question in order to make a sound selection from investment alternatives.

Besides providing a company's financial statements, the typical annual report contains other valuable information. Some companies are more forthcoming in their annual reports than others. An important section to read is the president's report to shareholders, which covers highlights of the past year, comments on the outlook for the current year and discusses such items as expansion plans, management and product changes. The annual report also may include comparative operating and financial statistics for the past ten years, information on the various segments of the company's business, graphs and pictures of the company's plants, products and services.

Assets: what the company owns

Liabilities: what the company owes

Owner's Equity: the worth or the value of the company

Assets = Liabilities + Owner's Equity

The core of the annual report is the balance sheet and earnings statement. The balance sheet breaks down the company's assets and offsetting liabilities, with the difference being the equity value of the company, which is owned by the shareholders.

The earnings statement shows how much revenue a company received during the year from the sale of its products or services and the expenses it incurred for wages, materials, operating costs, taxes and other expenses. The difference between the revenue and expenses is the company's profit or loss for the year.

Net Income = Revenue - Expenses

$$Earnings\ per\ common\ share\ =\ \frac{net\ earnings\ -\ any\ preferred\ dividends}{number\ of\ common\ shares\ outstanding}$$

Retained earnings = net income - any dividends

An important number from the shareholder's point of view is earnings per share, which is derived from the earnings statement. By expressing a company's net earnings in this way, the shareholder is able to see clearly how profitable their ownership interest in the company is and whether dividends are likely to be paid.

The only direct link between the earnings statement and the balance sheet is through what is called retained earnings. After a company figures its net profit, the so-called bottom line, it may pay a dividend to its shareholders. Any profit then left over is retained by the company and is added to the shareholders' equity on the balance sheet.

Sales

When assessing the outlook for a company's profitability, the first thing to consider is its ability to increase sales. Whether sales are increasing or decreasing, the trend should be analysed to isolate the main causes. For example, a rising trend may reflect such factors as increases in product prices or product volumes, the acquisition of a new company or a gain in market share, or an upswing in the business cycle. By isolating the main factors affecting sales, you are better able to judge whether the trend will continue into the future.

Operating Costs

The next step is to look at operating costs to assess the overall efficiency of operations. Just because operating costs go up doesn't mean a company is in trouble; it's normal for these costs to rise as sales increase. What's important is whether operating costs as a percentage of sales is rising, stable or declining. A rising trend over several years may indicate that a company is having difficulty keeping overall costs under control, which would hurt its profitability. A falling trend suggests that a company is becoming more cost effective, which should help profits.

Again it's important to consider the main reasons for changes in operating costs. Although these may be difficult to determine, they are important in understanding what affects the company's cost structure. Factors that can affect operating costs include the cost to the company of its raw materials, the introduction of more efficient equipment, or an increase in wage payments. Finally, toward the bottom of the earnings statement is the company's net after-tax profit or loss. Regardless of whether this is up or down in the latest year, what matters is the trend over several years. One way to assess this trend is by comparing the net profit as a percentage of sales, called the net profit margin, over a number of years. This provides a quick reference to the ability of management to produce profits.

Analysts use a number of other financial ratios to judge how well management makes use of a company's resources. One common ratio is the return on equity, which indicates management's effectiveness at increasing profitability in relation to the equity capital of the company. A declining trend reveals for shareholders that their investment is being employed less productively.

$$Net\ profit\ margin\ =\ \frac{net\ income\ -\ equity\ income\ +\ minority\ interest}{net\ sales}$$

$$Net\ return\ on\ equity\ =\ \frac{net\ income\ -\ preferred\ dividends\ (if\ any)}{common\ equity}$$

$$Inventory\ turnover\ ratio\ =\ \frac{cost\ of\ goods\ sold}{inventory}$$

Another measure of efficiency, and thus profitability, is the inventory turnover ratio, which is important for companies that carry substantial inventories, such as manufacturers and merchandisers. The ratio measures the number of times a company's inventory is turned over in a year. It may also be expressed as a number of days. A high turnover ratio is considered desirable, because this requires a smaller investment in inventory than a company that produces the same sales with a low turnover. There is no standard yardstick for this ratio, as inventory turnover rates vary greatly from industry to industry.

Investors who focus on a company's potential to generate superior earnings are known as growth investors. As future earnings grow, goes the reasoning, so will the price of the company's shares. Other investors, instead, look for value when buying a stock. They ask, is the market pricing a particular stock too cheaply? This value can be measured in a number of ways. Usually when we think of securities having yields we think of interest rates on bonds. But stocks have yields too, based on their dividend payouts, expressed as a percentage of the share price. Dividend yields represent the investor's percentage return on an investment at its prevailing market price, and enable the investor at least superficially to compare shares of different companies. The problem is that dividend yields don't reveal some important aspects of a company, such as the quality and record of its management. Also, it's important to remember that some stocks have high dividend yields because the share price has dropped off, perhaps for good reason.

$$current\ yield\ =\ \frac{annual\ dividend}{current\ market\ price}\ X\ 100$$

$$P/E\ =\ \frac{current\ market\ price}{earnings\ per\ share}$$

Probably the most widely used measure of a stock's value is the price-to-earnings, or P/E, ratio. This provides a comparison between different stocks by creating a ratio of the market price of each stock relative to its earnings per share. The P/E ratio, which is only calculated for common shares, is a useful measurement because it reflects the views of thousands of investors on the quality of the issue. However, P/E ratios of different stocks can only be compared when the companies are in the same line of business; each industry tends to have its own P/E ratio level that is considered normal. But even this norm can change, rising usually when the overall market is going up, and falling when the market is in retreat.

Value investors look for low P/E ratios, which could signal that a stock is undervalued by the market. Growth investors, on the other hand, are more comfortable with high P/E ratios, because they expect a company's earnings will grow at a fast enough rate to justify paying a relatively high market price. There is no standard P/E ratio. Still, we can safely say that stable industries such as banks and utilities tend to have low P/E ratios, whereas more speculative investments such as gold mining and communication stocks would have higher ratios.

Balance Sheet

Now that we've discussed how analysts make use of a company's earnings statement to evaluate its stock, let's look at what a typical balance sheet can reveal to the potential investor. Companies sell shares to the public to finance their business operations. Many companies also issue debt securities and take out bank loans to further expand their operations and add flexibility to their financing. A careful investor will keep a close eye on the amount and type of debt a company has in order to assess its financial health. A company with too much debt runs the risk of having its profits eaten away by interest charges when business slows down. On the other hand, having too little debt is seen as not making efficient use of the company's assets, with the result that profits are lower than they could be.

Obviously a big company will have more debt than a small one. So how do we know how much debt is too much?

This is one of the things we can learn by analysing a company's balance sheet. To start, we'll look at its structure.

A balance sheet has three main sections. On one side are listed the company's assets, including current assets, such as inventories, which can be turned into cash relatively easily. Then there are fixed assets, usually buildings and machinery that are not intended to be sold. These and various other asset categories are offset by the company's liabilities, which are listed on the other side of the balance sheet. Included here are current liabilities, which are debts due within a year or those that a company incurs in the ordinary course of doing business, such as unpaid bills. Another liability is long-term debts, which come due more than a year in the future. Typical long-term debts are mortgages, bonds and debentures. As we mentioned, the difference between a company's assets and its liabilities is the equity value of the company that is owned by the shareholders. The Shareholders' Equity section of the balance sheet usually appears under the Liabilities, so that one side of the balance sheet equals the other.

*So I suppose that's why they call it a **balance** sheet.*

That's right, Pat. But what do you **do** with the information on a balance sheet? First, we can gauge a company's liquidity, which is a colourful term for its ability to access funds readily.

Liquidity is something every company needs in order to meet its obligations, expand its volume of business and take advantage of financial opportunities. A lack of liquidity is a frequent cause of business failure.

A company's liquid assets are referred to as working capital, which is simply the difference between the current assets and current liabilities on the balance sheet. As an analytical tool, however, the investor is interested in a calculation known as the working capital ratio. This is arrived at by dividing a company's current assets by its current liabilities. A ratio of 2:1, for example, reveals that a company has $2.00 in current assets to pay for each $1.00 of current liabilities. As a rule of thumb, a 2:1 working capital ratio is considered a minimum, although this can vary, depending on the type of business. Working capital ratios also can be too high. A ratio that consistently runs above 5:1 could indicate the company has excess inventory that it can't sell, or perhaps that its management is overly cautious. A more stringent gauge of a company's liquidity is known as the quick ratio, or simply as the acid test. In this test, a company's inventories, which are sometimes difficult to turn into ready cash, are excluded from current assets before doing the working capital ratio calculation. What's left then in current assets is just actual cash and other quick assets, such as government treasury bills. There is no standard for this ratio, although a company is generally considered to be in a good liquidity position if it has at least $1.00 in quick assets for every $1.00 in current liabilities. However, some companies may be just fine with a quick asset ratio of less than one-to-one if they have a high rate of inventory turnover.

$$\text{working capital or current ratio} \ = \ \frac{\text{current assets}}{\text{current liabilities}}$$

$$\text{quick ratio} \ = \ \frac{\text{current assets - inventories}}{\text{current liabilities}}$$

Couldn't a company have plenty of liquidity but still have too much debt to pay back sometime in the future?

Yes. And to understand this we need to look at a company's debt in relation to its total capitalization. As we discussed, a company gets its capital from various sources, including retained earnings, common shareholders, preferred shareholders, which are all part of Shareholder's Equity, and bank loans and other debt instruments. The conscientious investor wants to know how much of a company's total capitalization can be made up of debt without setting off warning bells.

$$\% \text{ of debt in capital structure} \ = \ \frac{\text{total debt}}{\text{total debt } + \text{ equity}} \ X \ 100$$

Unfortunately, there is no easy answer for this. The relationship of debt to total capitalization varies widely for companies in different industries. For example, it is normal for public utility, pipeline and real estate companies to have a big proportion of their capital structure made up of debt. But if a company that manufactures products subject to wide fluctuation in demand has as much debt in its capital structure as does a public utility, the soundness of its capital structure would be questioned. Analysts use a certain amount of intuition in judging what is acceptable capitalization. But as a rule of thumb industrial companies' capital should be limited to at most one-third debt.

$$debt/equity \quad = \quad \frac{total\ debt}{shareholders'\ equity}$$

Another way of looking at levels of debt is by means of the debt-to-equity ratio. As its name implies, this test measures a company's total debt as a proportion of shareholders' equity. This is a key measure that can serve as a warning that a company's borrowing is excessive; the higher the ratio, the higher the financial risk. Again there is a rule of thumb, which must be applied flexibly. Industrial companies' debt should be at most half the value of the equity.

Finally, let's see how we can evaluate a company's ability to service its debt, that is, pay the annual interest costs. This ratio, known as interest coverage, indicates how many times the interest charges or expenses are covered by earnings available to pay them. Again, there is no single correct answer. The proper coverage varies from industry to industry, and from company to company, depending on their past earnings records and future prospects. Generally speaking, however, an industrial concern's interest charges should be covered at least three times over by its earnings available to pay them. It's important that interest coverage is consistently above minimum levels. You should examine this coverage for each of a company's preceding five years.

$$Interest\ Coverage \quad = \quad \frac{net\ income - equity\ income + minority\ interest + all\ taxes + all\ interest\ charges}{all\ interest\ charges}$$

No matter how carefully you analyse a stock, there's always a risk that something inside the company, in the economy or in the political world could derail the best laid investment plans. There are certain strategies that can be used to help minimize such risks, especially for a first-time investor.

Diversification

The first is, don't put all your eggs in one basket: diversify your stock holdings. Let's say world oil prices plummet while you're holding stock in an energy company. Suddenly you're a lot poorer, at least on paper. But you probably wouldn't feel quite as bad if you also held shares in a company that benefited from low oil prices, such as a transportation concern. That's diversification. Even owning some bonds could offset the negative consequences of holding too narrow a selection of stocks. In the example above, bonds might be expected to rally if oil prices fall, because of reduced inflationary pressures in the economy. A problem with diversifying is that it costs more money to buy a variety of stocks than to buy shares in just one or two companies. Not every investor has the ability to build up a sufficiently diversified portfolio of stock holdings. It's a good idea to talk to a professional advisor about creating the right investment portfolio to suit your needs, and how much this will cost.

Dollar Cost Averaging

	$ Invested	Price	Shares
Jan.	200	$10	20
Feb.	200	$8	25
March	200	$9	22.22
April	200	$12	16.67
Totals	800		83.89

Average price: $9.75

Average cost per share: $9.54

One thing that stymies nearly all investors at some point is picking the right time to buy or sell a stock. If you bought $5,000 worth of stocks one day and the market corrects 10% the next week, we'd say your timing was bad. How do you prevent this from happening? One way is with a discipline known as dollar cost averaging. This involves investing about the same amount of money at regular set intervals over a period of time. The funds should be invested in securities that represent reasonable value. By taking prices as they come, you sometimes pay more and sometimes less. When you pay more, less shares are purchased, since the amount invested each time is the same. So over a period of years you will pay an average price that normally is more favourable than if purchases are made at random intervals.

Dollar cost averaging requires some fortitude; you must have the courage to continue buying even during market declines. Although dollar cost averaging doesn't solve the problem of *what* to buy, it offers one solution as to *when* to buy.

Financial analysis doesn't stop once you choose the stocks for your portfolio. Companies should be continuously monitored for changes that might alter investment quality. One way to do this is to carefully read a company's quarterly financial statement which is distributed to shareholders and to the financial media. Also, if a company plans to issue new shares or debt securities, it will file a prospectus with the regulatory authorities that can contain new information of material importance. Besides monitoring developments at specific companies, you should also keep abreast of general economic trends, the anticipated direction of the business cycle, and various government policies that might affect investments.

Next week we'll look at some other investment possibilities. Equities are the major source of long-term capital growth, but there are different ways to buy them and there is a whole world of derivative products based on them. Knowing about these choices will help you make better investment decisions whatever asset class you go for.

See you then.

Summary

Besides borrowing money, issuing equity or shares is the other way companies raise funds: debt and equity are the major components of a company's capital structure. Common shares have a number of characteristics that appeal to investors: they carry a vote, they can appreciate in value, they can be easily bought or sold on a stock exchange or over-the-counter market, and they might pay dividends. Preferred shares do not carry a vote but they do pay a fixed dividend ahead of the common shares. Preferred shares have some characteristics in common with debt issues: they are both fixed-income investments and could have features such as sinking or purchase funds, various protective provisions, and a conversion, retraction or redemption feature.

Rights and warrants are issued by companies and allow investors to purchase shares at a stated price for a stated period of time. Rights are given to existing shareholders and warrants form part of a new issue of preferred shares or debentures. They both subsequently trade on stock markets. Investors will buy rights or warrants rather than the shares themselves because of the leverage potential: given a certain price increase in the stock, the right or warrant will show a greater percentage gain than the stock itself.

Much attention has been paid to evaluating and choosing stocks. Technical analysis looks at a stock's price movements to predict future trends. Fundamental analysis focuses on a company's financial position and earnings. As a starting point, it tries to identify industries with good prospects for growth, and then picks the best companies within those industries. A company's annual report is a good source of information. Besides management reports and a breakdown of the company's operating structure, it contains the company's balance sheet and earnings statement. These statements provide the data that is needed to calculate certain ratios that can be used to evaluate the company's profitability and operating efficiency. Other figures from these statements can be used to determine whether the company's shares are trading at an attractive price.

Whatever the analytic technique used, there is no guarantee that a company that scores well on the analysis will do well in reality. Diversifying investments among different companies, different types of companies, and different types of investments can soften the effect of one poor choice. Investing the same amount of money in one company's shares at regular intervals, a technique known as dollar cost averaging, can solve the problem of when to buy, and will also lower the average share cost.

Chapter 5
Investment Options

Everything you wanted to know about options but didn't know who to ask.

So now that I know all about securities themselves, let's get into something a little more aggressive! I want to speculate. I've heard a lot about options and how they can make you a millionaire almost overnight.

Well, I don't want to be a millionaire overnight – I don't want to speculate. I want to make my money work for me. I like nice steady returns and I want to minimize potential risk. Maybe I should just sit this lecture out and do some more in-depth research into income-producing securities.

Options can satisfy the requirements you both have – one for speculation and one for income, as well as a lot of other investment goals too. Options and other similar securities provide knowledgeable users with alternatives. Instead of simply buying a stock, a bullish strategy, you could buy a call or a bull call spread instead; even create a synthetic long stock or synthetic long calls. Options strategies can provide you with profitable alternatives to investing in actual stocks and bonds that are more appropriate to help you accomplish your goals. But as Pat suggests, options may not be for everyone. It takes some time to be knowledgeable enough to use these products successfully.

Now Enzo – this seems to be getting a little complicated – synthetic stock positions? I think these products could very well be over my head.

The main problem with options and similar derivative instruments is that investors don't learn enough of the basics before they jump into the market. And without that knowledge, these products can be dangerous. They can offer significant leverage to the novice investor, but leverage is a two-edged sword. You have to understand this product's power before investing.

I've read a great deal about the problems that can be caused by options and derivatives. Are these products simply another fad similar to junk bonds?

Actually options have been around for a long time. Some say they were in use as a financial product as far back as ancient Egypt, but well-documented claims as to their use date back to the tulip mania in Holland in the seventeenth century. But how and where they came about really isn't the issue. The question really is: what can options do for you, the investor?

In 1634-37, a mania to possess tulips swept through Holland. When speculation crashed to a halt in 1637, it took the Dutch economy many years to get over the side effects.

Learning the Basics

There is a language that is unique to the options market. Although some terms may already be familiar to you, to fully understand and utilize options properly, you must be familiar with the proper terminology and be able to use these terms in discussing potential strategies with your Investment Advisor.

An option itself does not represent a tangible, physical thing in the same way a stock or bond represents ownership or money owing. An option is really just a contract or agreement between two parties – a buyer and a seller. This contract clearly specifies all the details of the agreement including what the contract is based on and how long it is to be in force. You can buy and sell these contracts just as you can buy and sell other securities.

More importantly, options can add choice and dimension to your portfolio. By purchasing an option, you can achieve a high degree of exposure with a limited and known risk level. Selling options in conjunction with ownership of the underlying security can provide or improve its income potential. And options also provide flexibility. By mixing and matching various options positions, you can create a vast number of strategies, to take advantage of pricing anomalies or to generate a position that reflects a complicated and personal view of the market.

What is an Option?

As the word *option* connotes, an option is about choice. It offers opportunities to the average investor that were never available before.

Say you believe the markets are overpriced and there may be a selloff. Now you can sell the market as represented by an index in one transaction – by purchasing an index put – in a dollar amount suitable to your own circumstances. Maybe you think the Japanese yen is going to stage a rally – want to participate? It's as easy as buying a call on the yen. Do interest rates look like they are destined to rise? Buy puts on bonds. Now you can take advantage of your opinion to either protect your assets or to gain from your unique insights and trade an option product that will reflect *your* opinion.

Options have been available to investors for many years but were traded over-the-counter until 1973. At that time the Chicago Board Options Exchange, or CBOE, began to trade options in a public marketplace similar to a stock exchange. This new marketplace was developed as a hybrid market that used some of the best features of the stock market and the commodities market to create a unique listed product – the option. Options had some notoriety prior to 1973, and the OTC marketplace was, for the average investor, inefficient, with poor liquidity and poor visibility. The organized option market solved these two problems and created an efficient marketplace for large and small investors alike. Since 1973, options have been listed on indexes, currencies, bonds, interest rates, as well as precious metals and commodity futures.

As mentioned earlier, an option is an agreement between two parties, the buyer and the seller. The buyer pays a fee or *premium* to the seller, to purchase the right to buy or sell a specific item or security. This item or security upon which the contract is based is called the underlying security or underlying interest, and can be any one of a variety of things. There are options based on equities, indexes, bonds, actual interest rates, currencies and precious metals. The seller of the option receives a premium and takes on the obligation of fulfilling the rights granted to the buyer. The option has a limited lifespan, called the *time to expiry,* which can be anywhere from one day to three years – the greater the lifespan of the option contract, the greater the premium or value of the option. The expiry of an equity option occurs on the Saturday following the third Friday of the month specified in the contract. Expiration of options on other products may be at different times so you should check with your IA before an order to buy an option is given.

Puts and Calls

There are two types of options: puts and calls. The put option allows the holder to **sell** the underlying interest, while the call option allows the holder to **buy** the underlying interest at the strike price, either at expiration or at any time prior to the expiration of the contract. If the buyer of an option decides to *exercise* the right to buy or sell the underlying interest or security, the transaction would be done at the price specified in the contract. This price is called the *strike* or *exercise price.* Some options can be exercised at any time before their expiration date. Such options are called *American-style* or simply *American* options. Options listed on individual shares, or equity options, are American-style and can be exercised at any time, resulting in either the purchase or sale of the security on the day the option is exercised. Other options are *European,* which means that you cannot exercise the option until just prior to its expiry. Most, but not all, index options are *European-style.*

What an Option Looks Like

Stocks and bonds are issued by companies to investors, and ownership is evidenced by a certificate. While most investors may never actually see a stock or bond certificate, ownership of that security is registered with the company itself. The money from the original issue of securities was received by the company to use as it saw fit.

Clearing Corporations

Options, however, are not issued by the company but are *derived* from existing securities. They are called *derivative* securities. The money generated by the issue of the option goes directly to its writer. The option contract between the buyer and the writer is actually issued by a third party to the transaction, the clearing corporation which was set up specifically by the exchanges that deal in options for the purpose of maintaining records of all listed options trading. The clearing corporation ensures that for each option buyer, there is an option seller. It guarantees the fulfilment of each contract, so there is never a risk of default once the listed option is issued to the buyer and seller. All that evidences ownership of an option is the contract, which is printed by the broker arranging the buy or sell, as well as the records maintained by the clearing corporation. The contract you receive looks similar to this example.

Option writer: the creator or originator of the contract

Sample Only   ABC Brokerage Ltd.
                           Address

As agents, we have for your account:

Bought 5   Opening Transaction   ACME   January 40 put @ 2.00 $1,000.00

                                                    Commission: 50.00
                                                    Total: $1,050.00

Account # 00-555-0   Sales Code 15

   Tanya Lee
   121 Park Street   Transaction Date: 05-20-XX
   Big Town, Your Province   Settlement Date: 05-21-XX
   XXX-XXX   EXCH: XXX

You should review the contract closely to ensure that all details are correct. Mistakes can occur and should be dealt with promptly, as options have a limited lifespan. Once they have expired, it is difficult to rectify any problems that might have occurred when the trade was done. You should retain all contracts for income tax purposes. Of particular importance to the investor are the following details listed on the contract.

(i)   the type of option – *put* or *call?*

(ii) the *month* and *strike price*

(iii) the *underlying security*

(iv) was the trade a *buy* or *sell?*

(v)   was the trade an *opening* or *closing transaction?*

If you are unsure of any aspects or terms listed on a broker's contract, contact your IA and get clarification.

Two items on the contract have not yet been discussed.

One is whether the contract was an opening or closing transaction. An initial trade is an opening transaction. For example, in the contract shown above, the investor purchased a put. This was an initial trade. If we assume that the investor, at some point in the future, decides to sell the put, it would be a closing transaction and all rights and obligations granted in the first trade would be cancelled.

Another item on the contract that would appear on opening sales only is the term *covered* or *uncovered*. These terms affect margin requirements and will be discussed later in the strategy portion of our talk. You should ensure that both opening / closing and covered / uncovered notations reflect your position. Discuss all differences or errors with your IA.

More Terminology

One of the big problems with option investing and subsequently developing strategies is the jargon used by IAs and investors alike. It is impossible to get away from this jargon though, and we should learn a few more terms. Some synonymous terms are:

> *writing is the same as an opening sell*
>
> *naked is the same as uncovered*
>
> *strike price is the same as exercise price*
>
> *premium is the same as price of the option*

Other terms used frequently when discussing options are: *time value* and *intrinsic value.*

The premium of an option is the price as determined by the marketplace. This price can be broken into two components – time value and intrinsic value. The following table illustrates some of the options that could be listed on the well-known stock, ACME Manufacturing.

Time value and intrinsic value calculations for options are the same as those for rights and warrants

C = call P = put	ACME market price: $40 PREMIUMS		
Strike prices	2-month	5-month	8-month
35 C 35 P	5.50 .35	6.50 1.00	8.00 1.50
40 C 40 P	2.50 1.75	3.50 2.00	4.75 2.25
45 C 45 P	.75 5.25	1.25 5.75	1.50 6.00

If you were to purchase an ACME five-month 35 call at a price of $6.50, you would be purchasing an option with an *intrinsic value* of $5. The underlying stock trades at $40; you could buy the call, exercise your right to buy the stock at $35, and then sell the stock at $40, for $5 more than you paid for it. So that call is worth at least $5. But this right to buy the stock at $35 can be exercised at anytime until the call's expiry. The stock *could* continue to go up in value. This five-month time period has to be worth something to an investor. To calculate the *time value* of the call, you subtract the intrinsic value, $5 in this case, from the market price of the call. The remaining premium value ($6.60 - $5.00) is $1.50 and is called the time premium or time value. It is the value investors place on the right to buy ACME Manufacturing stock at $35 per share for the next five months.

This leads to three new phrases: *in-the-money, at-the-money,* and *out-of-the-money.* The previous chart illustrates the application of these terms. If an option has intrinsic value, it is in-the-money by that amount. The $35 calls are in-the-money, as are the $45 puts. If an option has no intrinsic value, it is out-of-the-money. The $45 calls are out-of-the-money, as are the $35 puts. And if the strike price and market price of the underlying are the same, the option is at-the-money. The $40 calls and puts are both at-the-money.

While these terms are often used in discussing strategies, it is not necessary to memorize these descriptions in order to invest and trade options successfully.

So there are puts and calls, and you can buy or sell either one?

Yes, you can. Let's look at both the purchase and the sale of an option so you'll see what rights and obligations you would have.

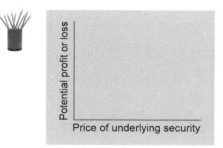

For all the options graphs that I'm going to show you, the horizontal axis represents the price of the underlying security, while the vertical axis represents the potential profit or loss on the position itself. The graphs do not take into account any time value that the option may have; only its intrinsic value is represented. This first graph illustrates only a call purchase on a stand-alone basis; in other words, assume you hold no other positions in the account.

The Call Buyer

The call buyer pays a premium for the right to *buy* the underlying security at the strike price anytime up until expiration of the option. The call buyer is bullish or is anticipating a rise in the price of the underlying security and will profit if the price of the stock rises. The maximum profit is theoretically unlimited, as it is possible that the stock could rise to infinity. The risk for the call buyer is limited only to the price paid for the call itself; that is, the premium.

The limited risk and unlimited profit characteristics of buying calls make them a popular choice among investors. In this graph, the underlying stock, ABC, trades at $30, while the call has a six month life with a strike price of $30.00.

The Call Buyer – *A Bullish Position*

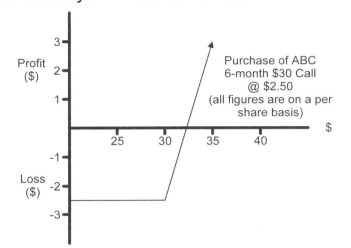

Purchase of ABC
6-month $30 Call
@ $2.50
(all figures are on a per share basis)

How to read this graph – *The call buyer stands to lose the entire premium paid for the option, (in this case – $2.50) if the market value of ABC is below $30 on expiration of the option. The investor breaks even at $32.50 and will participate dollar for dollar with any stock price movement once ABC rises above $32.50. Profit is unlimited, at least theoretically, as the price of the stock has no upside limitations.*

The Call Writer

The naked call writer receives a premium to take on the *obligation to sell the underlying security at the strike price anytime up until expiration of the option.* Call writers are neutral to bearish: they want to see the price of the underlying security fall in value or at least stay the same. The call writer has a maximum profit potential of the premium, and, like a short seller of stock, has unlimited risk. The stock can theoretically rise in value to infinity, and the writer could be required to purchase the stock at this inflated price, only to have to sell it at the strike price. Risk can be large and profits small.

Naked and Covered Writers

The naked writer does not own the underlying stock. The covered writer does.

The call writer's position can be illustrated as below, assuming that the call sold is on ABC, has a 90-day life and a strike price of $30. The market price of ABC is $30 and the call trades at $2.50. This is an aggressive strategy for an investor and should be considered as an alternative for those investors experienced in short selling.

The Naked Call Writer – *A Neutral Position*

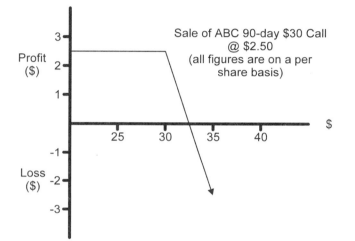

How to read this graph – *The naked call writer profits if the underlying security falls in value from current market prices. But profit is limited to the premium. Losses can be theoretically unlimited as the price of the underlying security can rise to infinity. The stock can rise in price to $32.50, the break even price, before the investor loses money. But after that point, the investor would lose dollar for dollar with any price movement in the stock.*

The Put Buyer

A put buyer obtains *rights for premiums paid.* A put buyer has the right to *sell* the underlying security at any time until the expiration day at the strike price stipulated in the contract. Put buyers are bearish or negative on the outlook for the underlying security and want to profit from decreasing market values.

The stock, ABC, is currently trading at $30 and the put being considered for purchase has a strike price of $30 and a time to expiration of approximately 90 days. The market price of the put is $2.00. This graph illustrates that the put buyer has a limited risk and a limited reward. The maximum profit to be made on the position is the exercise price of the put after costs and expenses. This is assuming that the stock falls to a price of zero.

The Put Buyer – *A Bearish Position*

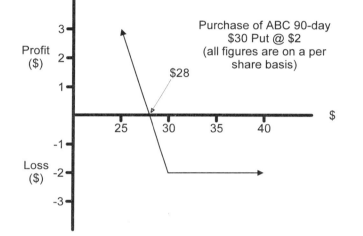

How to read this graph – *If the investor buys a put for $2.00, all that can be lost is $2, even if the stock rises to $40 or more. If the stock falls in value, the investor will break even (recoup the entire investment) at $28. If the stock continues to fall below $28, the investment will be profitable, doubling at $26. Maximum profit of $28 will occur at 0.*

The Put Writer

The put seller, or writer, on the other hand, takes on the obligation to *buy* the underlying security at the strike price until expiry, and receives a premium for his troubles. This obligation can be enforced at any time up until the expiration of the option. Put sellers are usually considered bullish to neutral, as they will profit if the underlying security stays above the strike or exercise price. The maximum profit that the put writer can make is the premium received from the sale of the put, and this maximum profit will be made if the put itself has little or no market value on the expiration day.

To illustrate how this position would compare to that of purchasing stock, let us assume that the stock, ABC, is still trading at $30. This time we are going to write a six-month put with a strike price of $30 and a premium of $3.00. The maximum profit, illustrated on the graph, occurs if the stock stays above $30: no-one would want to sell us their stock at $30 if it is worth more than that, and of course we would keep the premium of $3.00. If, however, the stock falls below $30, we would be forced to fulfil the obligation of buying the stock. Our worst case scenario would occur if the stock dropped all the way to zero; we would still be obligated to buy what was now a worthless stock at $30. Our loss would then be $30 less the $3 premium we had received, or $27.

The Put Writer – *A Bullish Position*

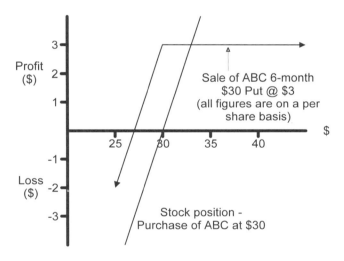

How to read this graph *– If the investor writes a put for $3, all that can be earned or made on the position is the $3 premium, even if the stock rises to $40. Because the $3 premium creates a cushion for the investor, the stock can fall to a price of $27 before there is any loss. If the stock continues to fall in value, the investor is at risk. The maximum loss occurs at $0. The investor is obligated to buy a worthless stock for $30. Because of the $3 premium received, the maximum loss would be $27 per share.*

Put writing is an aggressive strategy that may be quite profitable for an investor during buoyant markets, but should only be attempted if you can pay for the stock position that you might be obligated to buy. It is quite possible to assume too large a financial obligation because the money required to finance the position can be less than the alternative stock position. As well, the dollar amount of the premium can sometimes entice investors into taking on more risk than they can afford. This is one of the dangers of investing in options.

These four positions are the building blocks that the options investor can use to construct different investment strategies designed to protect assets, earn income, or participate in the price movement of various securities. If you understand these four positions clearly, with their attendant rights and obligations, designing a specific strategy becomes much easier.

The Four Basic Positions

- *buying calls*
- *writing naked calls*
- *buying puts*
- *writing puts*

It is often said that call buying and put writing or selling are comparable. While both strategies are bullish, they should not be considered to be interchangeable. Call buyers have rights, unlimited profit potential and limited risk. Put writers have limited profit potential and limited though substantial risk. Put writers have obligations, not rights. Call buying is an alternative to put selling, but is not a substitute. The same comparison exists with put buyers and call writers. The put buyer has rights, limited risk, and limited profit, although it can be substantial. The naked call writer has obligations, limited profit, and unlimited risk. The put buying strategy is an alternative to call writing but is not a substitute.

How Time Affects Options

One aspect to options trading that is sometimes misunderstood is the time factor and its influence on the price of an option. Options are wasting assets – they have a limited, preset lifespan and one day, sooner than the investor realizes, they will expire. Options have a time value, and as the expiry date for the option approaches, the time value decreases. Most investors wrongly assume that the cost of time is linear. So, if a three-month option had a time value of $1, then a six-month option would have a time value of $2.00. This linear interpretation of time value could be depicted graphically as:

A Linear Time Value Decay

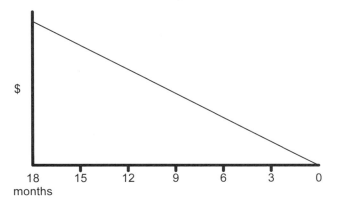

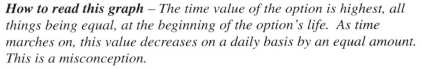

How to read this graph – The time value of the option is highest, all things being equal, at the beginning of the option's life. As time marches on, this value decreases on a daily basis by an equal amount. This is a misconception.

But time value is not linear – it decays on an *accelerated basis* in the final months and weeks, which looks more like:

How Time Value Really Decays

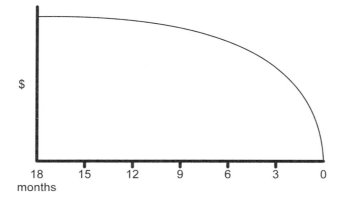

How to read this graph – *As previously illustrated, the time value of the option is highest at the beginning of the option's life. As time until expiry shortens, the time premium attributed to the option begins to decrease, with the most dramatic moves taking place in the final months and weeks before expiration.*

So the cost of a six-month option will be more than a four-month option; and the four-month option will be worth more than the two-month option, but not by the same amount. The time value of an option decreases very little over its lifetime, until about the three or four month mark; then it disappears quickly. It is vital to understand this time value decay, because taking advantage of this aspect of an option's price is essential to successful trading.

Often investors looking at the purchase of an option will choose the cheapest option, basing the investment decision on the actual dollar cost. As you can see from the preceding graph, time value decreases very rapidly as expiry approaches. Not only are you fighting the market, hoping that events will occur as forecast, but you are also fighting the clock. So buying the cheapest option with only a few weeks of life left is a fool's game. In choosing which option to buy or sell, time must be as important a consideration as the cost.

Time value, then, affects the price of an option – the longer the time to expiry, the greater the value of the option. Other factors that affect option prices are interest rates, dividends on the underlying common shares and, of course, the relationship of the strike price of the option to the stock price. Another important factor is the volatility of the underlying stock's market price. The following chart indicates how each of these factors would affect an option's price if that factor itself changed. An understanding of how each of the factors really relates to the option is beyond the scope of our talk tonight, but understanding the results of any changes in these factors is important.

Factors Affecting Options Premiums

	Put Premium	Call Premium
Interest Rates **Up**	⇧	⇧
Interest Rates **Down**	⇩	⇩
Dividend Yield **Up**	⇧	⇩
Dividend Yield **Down**	⇩	⇧
Volatility **Up**	⇧	⇧
Volatility **Down**	⇩	⇩

Using Options as Investment Vehicles

To really understand options, you should look at some of the strategies that can be implemented. By calculating the investment parameters such as cost, potential return on capital invested and the amount of money at risk, the characteristics of each strategy, and under what market conditions it should work, can be clearly outlined. You can make your decision and choose your strategy on an informed basis.

Let's use two separate scenarios to illustrate the use of the four basic option positions. A final illustration on covered writing will complete our talk.

Setting the Stage

For all illustrations, the following assumptions apply:

- options are American-style;
- no dividends are payable on the stock;
- commissions are not included;
- income and other taxes are not accounted for;
- your account holds only the position under discussion;
- all returns are calculated over the time period discussed and are not annualized.

ACME option prices appeared in the table on page 98

Scenario One

You are bullish on ACME Co. stock, currently trading at $40. There are three possible strategies that are appropriate in this situation:

* buying the stock itself;
* buying ACME $40 calls; or
* selling ACME $40 puts.

Scenario One – *Bullish on ACME*

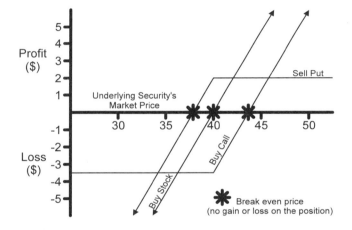

Strategy One – *Buy Stock*	Strategy Two – *Buy Calls*	Strategy Three – *Sell Puts*
Buy 500 ACME @ $40 Cost = $20,000	Buy 5 ACME 5-month 40 calls @ $3.50 Cost = $1,750	Sell 5 ACME 5-month 40 puts @ $2.00 Premium Received = $1,000 Margin Required = $5,000 (The credit received must stay in the account.)

A. Positive scenario - the stock rises in value by $4.00 over a 4-month time period.

Sell 500 ACME @ $44 Total Received .... $22,000 Less Cost .... $20,000 Profit............................. $2,000 Return 10%	Sell 5 5-month 40 calls @ $6.25 Total Received ....$3,125 Less Cost........................$1,750 Profit ....$1,375 Return 79%	Buy 5 5-month 40 puts at $0.25 (to close out position) Total Paid .... - $125 Plus Premium .... $1,000 Profit .... $875 Return 17.5%

B. Negative scenario - stock drops in value by $4.00 over a 4-month time period.

Sell 500 ACME @ $36 Total Received.............. $18,000 Less Cost .... $20,000 Loss .... - $2,000 Return .... - 10%	Sell 5 5-month 40 calls @ $0.50 Total Received .... $250 Less Cost..................... - $1,750 Loss ....$1,500 Return .... - 86%	Buy 5 5-month 40 puts @ $4.75 (to close out position) Total Paid .... $2,375 Plus Premium .... $1,000 Loss ....$1,375 Return .... - 27.5%

C. Typical scenario – nothing happens and the stock remains at $40. Time simply runs out on the options.

Sell 500 ACME @ $40 Total Received.............. $20,000 Less Cost .... $20,000 Balance .... 0 Return 0%	Sell 5 5-month 40 calls @ $1.00 Total Received .... $500 Less Cost........................$1,750 Loss ....$1,250 Return .... - 71.4%	Buy 5 5-month 40 puts @ $0.75 (to close out position) Total Paid .... $375 Plus Premium .... $1,000 Profit .... $625 Return 12.5%

Returns for Strategy Three are based on the deposit margin required, i.e. $5,000.

Summary

D. Dollar risk in the position:

Total Cost or $20,000 Per share = $40.00	Total Cost or $17,500 Per share = $3.50	Difference between the strike price and premium received ($20,000 less $1,000) or $19,000 Per share = $38.00

The total risk in all the positions occurs if the stock does not rise as expected and instead drops in price.

E. Maximum loss occurs at:

Zero - the stock cannot be sold and all capital is lost.	Below $40.00 - the call expires worthless.	Zero - the put is exercised and you must purchase the stock at $40.00. Your cost is $40 less the $2 premium, or $38.00.

F. Maximum Potential Reward:

Unlimited - the stock could rise to infinity.	Unlimited - the stock could rise to a price of infinity (but unlike the stock, the option eventually expires).	Limited - $1,000: the premium received.

There are some important differences between these three strategies. Buying stock is a long-term proposition. You can earn dividend income, if available, and participate in any rise in the security's price. Likewise, a drop in the security will create a loss, and the dollar risk amounts to the total cost price of the stock, or $20,000, if ACME dropped to zero. The long call position offers a great deal of leverage. There is a much lower dollar risk ($1,750 vs. $20,000), but the likelihood of losing all your money is greater. The call offers unlimited profit potential, but only for five months, and before you can participate dollar for dollar with ACME's price movement, the initial investment of $1,750 must be recouped. This occurs at $43.50. Of course, the leverage is that two-edge sword. The upside potential of the call is very attractive even with a small move in ACME's price. In this example, a 10% move equates to a return of 79% – not a bad return. Often novice investors will decide that with such attractive returns, they should invest an equal dollar amount, so that here, you would purchase closer to 55 contracts than five. If you normally buy 500 shares of stock, you are wiser to purchase five contracts, covering 500 shares. You should not overextend the leverage on the position, which could prove a fatal mistake.

The third strategy – writing puts – is quite a bit different from the other two, but does fit the overall parameter – it is bullish. This strategy performs even when the other strategies do not – when the stock's market price is flat. It is a short position – something similar to shorting stock, and carries with it a risk unlike that of the call strategy. There is a margin requirement to establish the position. The put writer *must be willing* to purchase the stock at the strike price if required to do so. That may mean that the stock could be at zero, yet the put writer must buy the stock at the $40 strike price. That is the risk in this strategy. When the writer least wants to buy the stock – there it is. Of course a writer can purchase the put at any time in the secondary market before it is exercised and close out the position. Once the put has been assigned or exercised, though, this recourse is not available.

If in fact the put writer was required to buy the stock because the holder exercised the put, there are still alternatives available. If the stock is thought of as a buy – the outlook still remains bullish or positive – the investor should simply hold the purchased stock for a price recovery. If further weakness looks possible, the stock should be sold and the loss taken before the price of the stock drops further. If the outlook is neutral to bullish, the strategy that is best employed would be the covered write – a hedging strategy popular with income-oriented investors that will be illustrated later on.

To sum up:

(i) The long stock position offers the investor income potential if dividends are paid, capital gains potential and returns commensurate with the price movement of the stock. Time is not a factor, for, barring any unforeseen events, the stock has no expiry.

(ii) The long call position offers leverage. For a portion of the cost of the long stock position, you can almost replicate the upside potential of the stock and at the same time severely limit the dollar risk. But, and it is a big but, time to expiry is a limiting factor.

(iii) The short put position offers income earning potential in neutral to bullish markets, and is levered, as the margin is less than the cost of the stock. Time is on your side, as the faster it runs out, the quicker the profit is booked. But risk is higher in this position – you have to monitor events carefully.

Scenario Two

Now you are bearish on ACME Co., still trading at $40 per share. You have three choices for an investment strategy:

- sell the stock short;
- buy a put on ACME; or
- write an ACME call.

Scenario Two – *Bearish on ACME*

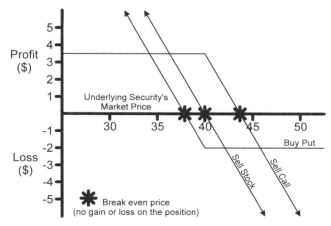

Strategy One – *Sell Stock Short*	Strategy Two – *Buy Puts*	Strategy Three – *Sell Calls*
Sell 500 ACME @ $40 Credit Received = $20,000 Margin Required = $6,000 (The credit received must stay in the account.)	Buy 5 ACME 5-month 40 puts @ $2.00 Cost = $1,000	Sell 5 ACME 5-month 40 calls @ $3.50 Credit Received = $1,750 Margin Required = $5,000 (The credit received must stay in the account.)

A. Positive scenario - the stock falls in value by $4.00 over a 4-month time period.

Buy 500 ACME @ $36	Sell 5 ACME 5-month 40 puts @ $4.00	Buy 5 ACME 5-month 40 calls @ $0.75
Total Cost .... -$18,000 Less Sale Proceeds ..... $20,000 Profit $2,000	Total Received .... $2,000 Less Cost .... $1,000 Profit $1,000	Total Received .... $1,750 Less Cost .... $375 Profit $1,375
Return 33%	Return 100%	Return 27.5%

B. Negative scenario - the stock rises in value by $4.00 over a 4-month time period.

Buy 500 ACME @ $44	Sell 5 ACME 5-month 40 puts @ $0.25	Buy 5 ACME 5-month 40 calls @ $4.75
Total Cost .... - $22,000 Less Proceeds .... $20,000 Loss .... - $2,000	Total Proceeds .... $125 Less Cost .... - $1,000 Loss .... - $875	Total Received .... $1,750 (from original sale) Less Cost .... $2,375 Loss .... - $625
Return .... - 10%	Return .... - 87.5%	Return .... - 12.5%

C. Typical scenario - nothing happens and the stock remains at $40. Time simply runs out.

Buy 500 ACME @ $40	Sell 5 5-month ACME 40 puts @ $0.25	Buy 5 5-month 40 calls @ $0.50
Total Received .... $20,000 Less Cost .... $20,000 Balance 0	Total Received .... $125 Less Cost .... $1,000 Loss $875	Total Received .... $1,750 Less Cost .... $250 Profit $1,500
Return 0%	Return .... - 87.5%	Return 30%

Returns for Strategies One and Three are based on the deposit margin required.

Summary

D. Dollar risk in the position:		
Unlimited	Total Cost or $1,000	Unlimited

The total risk in all the positions occurs if the stock does not fall as expected and instead rises in price.

E. Maximum loss occurs at:		
Infinity - theoretically the stock can rise to infinity.	$40 and above - the put expires worthless.	Infinity - theoretically the underlying stock can rise to infinity.

F. Maximum Potential Reward:		
$40 per share or $20,000 - or the total value of the stock if its market price falls to zero.	$40 per share less the cost of the put if the market price of the stock falls to zero by expiry.	$3.50 per share if the price of the stock falls below $40 by expiry.

Scenario Two also has some important differences between its three strategies. Selling stock short is an aggressive strategy that should only be attempted by those investors *willing* and *able* to accept the risks involved. Maintaining the short position for extended periods of time is expensive in terms of interest lost on capital, and dividends, which must be paid by the short seller. It could be years before the market realizes that a particular stock is overvalued. The put strategy offers the investor a limited risk position with much the same characteristics as the short stock position. While participation in terms of falling stock prices is initially curtailed because of the cost of the put, which must first be recouped, its risk limitations and non-responsibility for dividends make buying a put an attractive alternative to short selling.

The short call, on the other hand, is very similar to the short stock position, as risk is unlimited. There is a cushion of $3.50 per share, the premium of the call. If the stock begins to rise, you won't lose capital until the stock rises above $43.50. Another risk is, of course, the payment of a dividend on the stock. It is possible that a call writer may be exercised for the dividend payment. This is a risk that should be discussed at length with your IA. One advantage writing a call does have over the short sale of the stock itself is that the stock can remain static and the short call position will still be profitable.

To sum up:

(i)   The short stock position offers the investor capital gains potential commensurate with the market price of the security. Time is not a factor, but risks are substantial. Dividends and margin calls are also risks that cannot be fully determined in advance.

(ii) Buying a put offers the investor leverage. For a portion of the margin required for the short position, you can almost replicate the profit potential of the short stock position and at the same time limit the dollar risk to the premium only. Time is a limiting factor.

(iii) The short call position more closely replicates the short stock position, in that risk on the upside is in lock-step with the short stock position once the break-even price has been reached. But profit is *very* limited. This is a position in which time is working for you. This strategy is suitable for downward movements in the underlying stock's price. Risk is very high and the position should be monitored closely.

Covered Writing

Another strategy that doesn't really fit in with the previous examples is covered call writing. This conservative strategy takes advantage of that same accelerated decay in time premiums which can so work against an option buyer. While gains are possible, the potential is not as great as buying and trading options positions, but you can maintain an attractive level of return even in bear markets.

The covered write involves:

(i) buying (or holding) the underlying security

(ii) writing a call against this position

So, on one hand, you own the stock, and, on the other, you have the potential obligation to deliver it at the strike price. Covered writing allows you to maintain an investment and receive any income derived from it while taking advantage of the options market.

Covered call writing is a balancing act that can smooth out returns over the long run. The investor who writes consistently against the portfolio may not experience the peak of the market in terms of return; but also should not suffer the full extent of the lows. There is a premium cushion that softens the effect of tumbling market prices.

To illustrate:

You own 500 shares of ACME at a $40 cost price. You want to continue holding the stock, but you would like to earn some money now and decide to sell or write a call, using the five month 40 calls @ $3.50.

The following graph illustrates this position:

The Covered Write - *A Neutral Position on ACME*

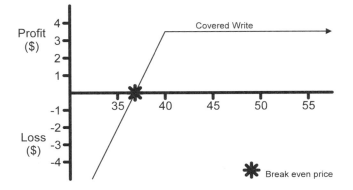

The first characteristic you must realize is the risk in the position is really in the stock position. Since you own the stock, the risk of losing money depends on what happens to its market price. The total risk is equal to the cost of the stock. This dollar risk is reduced by the premium received from the sale of the call, in this case $3.50 per share. So risk is $40 (the stock's cost) less $3.50, or $36.50 per share. The total dollar risk is equal to $36.50 x 500 or $18,250. The potential profit on this position is limited, as the call could obligate you to sell the underlying position any time until expiration. For this obligation you would receive $3.50 per share or $1,750 for 500 shares. The return can be calculated as

$$\frac{\$1,750}{18,250} \quad = \quad 9.6\%$$

If the stock falls in price, you would not have to worry about losing any money until it reached a price of $36.50. Below that price you would participate in further price declines in the stock. If the stock rises above the strike price of $40, you would not participate at all, unless you bought the call back and closed the trade out.

Whew! There's a lot more to options than I thought. I can see that I should consider doing some more homework.

You're right – we've barely touched the surface! And we've only talked about listed equity options. There are many more strategies and products to consider when investing in options. One way to begin to really understand the product is to chart both a number of listed options and their underlying security; this will help you get a better understanding of how options move in relation to the stock.

I'm intrigued by that last strategy – covered writing. It could work for me as I'm pretty conservative.

Yes, covered writing is a popular strategy, and, by choosing a strike price above the underlying security's market price, you can be more aggressive. By lowering the strike price, the strategy becomes more conservative.

How can we get started?

Well, you'll need to choose an IA who is registered to trade options, knowledgeable, and helpful. I also have some guidelines I use for my investing that can help.

Guidelines for Buying Options

- Make sure you thoroughly understand what is involved *before* you enter an order.
- Buy enough time for the idea to work. Don't be caught short on time.
- Establish a price for the option that *you* are willing to pay in terms of *risk*. Don't chase an option.
- Clarify goals and objectives before the trade is initiated. Establish your breakeven price in advance in case the market goes against you.
- Consider carefully the risk or leverage you are assuming – don't buy more than you can afford to lose.
- Be objective and flexible – consider all alternatives.
- Diversify into different underlying securities.
- Maintain a disciplined approach to trading.

Guidelines for Covered Writing

- Choose the stock, not the return.
- Write options with three to six months left until expiry.
- Be flexible – adjust the strategy if the stock price moves sharply.

- If the outlook on the stock changes to negative – close out both the stock and option position, as your short call will not compensate for a loss in share value.

- You may be forced to sell the stock – are you prepared for that?

Other products that may look and act like options are convertible preferreds and convertible debentures. If you strip away the preferred or debenture part of the security, what remains is the conversion privilege, which is like a call option. And the astute investor will use the options market to price such conversion features.

Tonight we've simply described the more commonplace option products – those based on equities. Other products include options on bonds, currencies, indexes, commodity futures, and silver and gold too. You can also find option-like characteristics embedded in other investment vehicles, such as convertible preferreds and debentures. And while you may never trade a listed option, the likelihood of trading a vehicle with an embedded option is high. I hope that tonight's talk will help you invest in these products with more understanding and skill.

Summary

Options are derivative products — they derive from another security, often a stock. They allow you to buy or sell a stock or other type of security at a fixed price for a fixed period of time. They usually trade for more than their intrinsic value, as investors are willing to pay for the leverage potential over a period of time. In these respects they resemble rights and warrants, but there are some differences too. Options are issued by a third party rather than by the company that issued the underlying stock, and they trade on an options market rather than a stock market, although the options market may be situated on the stock market floor.

The option issuer is called the writer, the price of the option is its premium, and the price at which the stock can be bought or sold is the strike price. There are two types of options. A call gives you the right to buy shares at a certain price for a certain period of time, whereas a put lets you sell them. A call writer takes on the obligation to sell these shares if asked to do so, and a put writer must buy them if required. The option holder decides whether to exercise the option, sell it, or let it expire, and the option writer acts according to the holder's decision.

There are four basic options positions that an investor can undertake: buy a call, write a call, buy a put and write a put. Each reflects a certain outlook on the underlying stock, each can be used to accomplish certain goals and each has its own degree of risk and reward. Call writers who own the underlying security are known as covered writers, and their outlook, goals and risk-reward ratio differs from those of the naked call writer, who does not own the underlying stock. If the call is exercised, the naked writer would have to buy the underlying stock at its current price in order to sell it to the call holder.

Chapter 6
Managed Money

The class finds out how they can hire professionals to oversee their investments.

Tonight we're going to look at how you can get someone else to make your investment decisions. Many investors assume that going this route means that they don't need to learn about the markets and only need to be concerned about their portfolio at tax time. It doesn't work like that. You still have to choose who you are going to trust your money to and you still have to monitor their progress. In many cases you have to choose the asset class you want to invest in and you always have to choose which method of professional management you want to go with. We'll look at mutual funds and then at other money management plans.

Probably no other type of investment has received as much publicity as mutual funds. Even so, mutual funds are often misunderstood. And, if you want to avoid pitfalls later on, you should be aware of how mutual funds differ from each other before handing over your life savings.

Mutual funds are frequently the investment choice for first-time purchasers of securities. Canada's mutual fund industry has ballooned in recent years, largely because of a flood of new investors seeking a higher rate of return than that available from bank savings accounts and GICs. What began the decade as a $30 billion industry now holds about $220 billion of Canadians' savings. And this is expected to almost double by the turn of the century.

Why are mutual funds so popular? For one thing, they come in a variety of sizes and shapes. Through mutual funds, you can hold stocks or bonds, or a blend of the two as well as other investments such as real estate or money market funds. With a single investment, a mutual fund can offer a variety of securities in a number of different industries – a particular advantage for the small investor with insufficient resources to create a diversified portfolio. And mutual funds are professionally managed, so the mix of investments is regularly readjusted to suit current conditions.

It sounds really good. Where are the drawbacks?

Well, Pat, mutual funds aren't for everybody. Most funds emphasize long-term investment and thus are unsuitable for investors seeking spectacular short-term performance. You can double your money on a speculative penny stock in a few months if you pick the right one, but no mutual fund, with its diversified portfolio of securities, can offer that type of return. Funds that levy sales charges may also deduct these from the initial investment, which also makes purchasing a fund on a short-term basis unattractive. And even professional money managers can call the market wrong, resulting in a loss for the fund's investors.

Investing in a mutual fund means buying shares, or units, in the fund's assets, represented by its portfolio of securities. Mutual funds also are known as open-ended investment funds, because they continuously offer more shares for sale to the public. At the same time, you have the continuing right to withdraw your investment simply by submitting your shares back to the fund and receiving the current value per unit. This characteristic is known as the right of redemption, and it is the hallmark of mutual funds.

So does the price of the shares go up as more people buy? And just how much should we expect to pay for a mutual fund share?

No, the price doesn't depend on how many people are buying, but on the market value of the fund's portfolio. And here's where mutual funds differ from other securities. In the case of a mutual fund share, the price closely approximates the fund's NAVPS, or net asset value per share. In other words, if the fund were to liquidate all its securities at their current market value and pay off all its liabilities, the proceeds attributed equally among all the shares would be the net asset value per share. So even though a fund may issue more shares, that won't change the share price because the fund's assets have grown by the same proportion.

$$NAVPS = \frac{Assets\ (including\ investments)\ -\ Liabilities}{Number\ of\ shares\ outstanding}$$

Although there is no typical price for a mutual fund share, investors should be aware that they may be required to pay a sales charge, or to commit to paying a redemption fee when the shares are eventually sold. We'll discuss this in more detail later.

Choosing the right mutual fund depends on your investment goals and your ability to tolerate risk. Some investors become comfortable taking increasingly greater risks as their level of sophistication grows over time. With dozens of mutual fund companies, offering shares in hundreds of different funds, there is a wide range of choice from the safest money market investments to the riskiest overseas funds.

Do mutual funds have any form of government backing, similar to deposit insurance on bank accounts or to the Canadian Investor Protection Fund?

No they don't. As with buying stocks or bonds or other securities, the risk of price fluctuations you assume in buying mutual fund shares is all yours to bear. That's why it's important to choose the right fund to match your objectives and risk tolerance. On the other hand, the fund's assets are held by a custodian, not the fund company, so there is no danger of the manager absconding with your money or using it for questionable purposes. As well, the fund's assets are segregated from those of the custodian, and are protected by trust and banking laws. Finally, some of the provinces have set up contingency trust funds, which, although they have never been drawn upon, are available to investors in the event that fraudulent behaviour endangers their assets.

Mutual fund custodian: a chartered bank or trust company which holds the assets of a mutual fund.

Contingency trust funds have been set up in British Columbia, Nova Scotia, Ontario and Quebec.

To learn about a fund's investment goals, you should begin by reading the offering prospectus, which will describe the degree of safety or risk involved, whether the fund's prime objective is income or capital gain, and the main types of securities in its investment portfolio. A fund prospectus can either be obtained by contacting an Investment Advisor or by calling the mutual fund company directly. Business sections of most of the major daily newspapers publish monthly mutual fund surveys, some of which contain company phone numbers.

Many companies that offer a variety of mutual funds allow clients to transfer between funds without any additional charge. This gives you a convenient way to readjust your own portfolio of funds as market conditions and personal circumstances change.

Based on their differing investment objectives, there are a few main types of funds:

Income or Bond Funds

These funds emphasize safety of principal and high income. They invest mainly in good quality, high yielding government and corporate debt securities, some high-yield preferred and common shares and mortgages. Unit prices of income funds hold relatively steady when interest rates are stable, but they can move sharply during periods of interest rate volatility.

Mortgage Funds

Mortgage funds have investment goals similar to bond funds, and unit values are affected by similar economic factors. Fund investors hold a share in a group of mortgages, much as bond fund investors hold a share in a group of bonds, rather than holding title to a particular property.

Money Market Funds

These funds became popular with investors during the 1980s and early 1990s, and still represent one of the largest categories of mutual funds. They aim to achieve a high level of income and liquidity through investment in short-term money market instruments such as treasury bills, commercial paper and short-term government bonds. However, these funds have limited opportunity for capital gain. As a result, many funds keep the net asset value at a set level, typically $10, by distributing monthly income to unitholders in cash or new units.

Balanced Funds

Balanced funds have as their main investment objective a mixture of safety, income and capital appreciation. To achieve this, the funds hold a balanced portfolio of fixed income securities for stability and income, plus a broad group of common stock holdings for diversification, dividend income and growth potential. The balance between defensive and aggressive security holdings is rarely 50-50; rather, managers of balanced funds adjust the percentage of each part of the total portfolio in accordance with current market conditions and future expectations.

Common Stock or Equity Funds

These funds are primarily invested in common shares. Short-term notes or other fixed income securities may be purchased from time to time in limited amounts for diversification, income and liquidity. However, the bulk of the assets are in common shares in the pursuit of capital gain. Because common share prices are typically more volatile than other types of securities, net asset values of equity funds tend to fluctuate more widely than those funds previously mentioned. Some equity funds invest in a variety of overseas markets as well as Canada and the United States, looking for the greatest opportunity for growth on a global basis.

As with common stocks, equity funds range greatly in degree of risk and growth potential. Some are broadly diversified, heavily invested in blue-chip, income yielding common shares and may, therefore, be classified at the conservative end of the equity fund scale. Others adopt a more aggressive investment stance, seeking capital gains at the sacrifice of some safety and income.

Specialty Funds

Specialty funds are those which concentrate portfolio holdings on shares of a group of companies in one industry, in one geographic location or in one segment of the capital market. While still offering some diversification in their portfolios, they are more vulnerable to swings in the industry in whose shares they specialize. If the portfolio contains foreign securities, there also could be the risk of changes in currency values. Many specialty funds, but not all, tend to be more speculative than most types of common share funds.

Global Funds

These funds seek gains and diversification by investing in markets that offer the best prospects, regardless of location. Some global funds are invested in bonds, others are equity funds and still others are money market funds.

Dividend Funds

Dividend funds invest primarily in high quality preferred and some-times common shares of taxable Canadian corporations, in order to obtain maximum dividend income.

Real Estate Funds

These funds invest in income-producing property such as shopping centres in order to achieve long-term growth through capital apprecia-tion and the reinvestment of income.

Ethical Funds

Ethical funds make investment decisions based on moral criteria, which vary from fund to fund. One ethical fund may avoid investing in companies that profit from tobacco, alcohol or armaments, while another fund may invest according to religious beliefs.

With so many different funds around, how do I select a suitable one? Even after putting aside the specialty funds, there are hun-dreds of funds offering just plain vanilla Canadian stocks and bonds.

Advice from an Investment Advisor could help steer you through the mutual fund maze. Even so, an investor with the skills to judge a mutual fund on their own is better equipped to ask the right questions, and get the right answers, than an investor without such abilities. We've already discussed different types of funds, based on their invest-ment objectives. Now let's talk about how well they perform.

A good place to start is the mutual fund surveys published monthly in the business sections of many major newspapers. These provide valuable information on how a fund measures up against its peers. There is information on a fund's various fees, collectively known as the management expense ratio (MER), and on sales commissions, or loads. The tables show whether a fund is eligible for inclusion in a Registered Retirement Savings Plan. There also is data on each fund's historical rate of return over time periods of varying length. Typically, these show how the fund fared over the past one month, six months, one year, three years, five years and ten years.

As we know, history is no sure guide to the future. A fund with a bright past record could falter next week, especially if market conditions suddenly change. Conversely, a weak performing fund might prompt its management to change their investment approach, and the fund could emerge a winner. Still, looking at a fund's past performance, especially over an extended period of time, gives some idea of how well a fund manager has coped with diverse market conditions in the past.

When comparing performance records, it is important not to compare two funds that have different investment objectives, such as an equity and a fixed income fund. Behind a higher rate of return in an equity fund, for example, there is also a higher degree of risk. Comparisons with stock exchange indices, such as the TSE 300 Composite Index, also can be misleading. Unlike mutual funds, some stock market indices don't include the added returns from reinvesting dividends.

The TSE also has a Total Return Index, which does include reinvested dividends and could therefore be fairly compared to the return on an equity mutual fund.

I've seen advertisements for mutual funds. But I'm not sure how to go about buying them.

Buying Mutual Funds

There are three main ways that mutual fund companies market their shares to the public. Most companies sell their products through investment dealers and mutual fund sales companies. A few companies, including all the chartered banks, market their mutual funds directly to the public. The third marketing route is for each fund to have commissioned sales representatives. The main distinction between these methods is that dealers and commissioned sales representatives advise clients on which mutual funds best suit their personal investment goals and, in the case of a dealer, can offer funds from a variety of fund companies. Direct marketers, however, are not usually qualified to provide advice and will sell their own funds only.

Unlike stocks, which are generally bought in board lots of 100, mutual fund investments can be made without regard to how many shares are being purchased. Instead, you decide how much money you want to invest. The fund company then issues the corresponding number of shares, even if this involves fractions of shares. The only restriction is that fund companies normally set a minimum dollar amount that they will accept from investors as an initial lump sum purchase. Some large mutual funds have initial minimum purchase levels in the $200 to $1,000 range, but most require a minimum of $1,000. There also are minimum dollar amounts for subsequent cash purchases, perhaps in the $50 to $100 range.

Most mutual fund companies also have so-called accumulation purchase plans, which allow the investor to acquire additional shares in the fund on a periodic basis. Such plans might require a lower minimum initial investment than lump sum purchases.

Accumulation programs appeal to smaller investors who cannot make large cash investments all at once. They also appeal to individuals interested in dollar-cost averaging.

You can also can add to your holdings of mutual funds by allowing dividends paid by the funds to be reinvested. Many funds do this automatically unless otherwise instructed.

You said investment dealers and commissioned sales representatives provide advice on mutual funds. Is there a charge for this service?

Fees

Yes, there is. And it's well worth investigating such charges before buying a mutual fund. Direct marketers generally don't provide much investment advice, but, at the same time, the funds they sell usually don't carry a sales charge. They are known in the industry as no-load funds. Most no-load funds are sold by the big banks, which market their products through their vast branch networks, and by some independent companies. For investors who know just what they want, or for purchases of relatively straightforward products, such as money market funds, a no-load company might offer the best value.

But not everyone wants to make major investment decisions without the benefit of professional advice. After all, these decisions could affect your net worth. That's where dealers and commissioned sales representatives come in. A few percentage points in sales commissions today might be a small price to pay for making the most appropriate investment decisions.

There is no standard when it comes to mutual fund sales charges. Instead, they depend on the type of fund being purchased, the method of purchase, and the amount of money being invested. For the ordinary investor, however, a typical sales charge, also known as a front-end load when it is paid at the time of purchase, represents about 3% to 5% of the amount being invested. But don't necessarily be put off by a higher sales charge. The particular fund might be worth it.

The last few years have brought a sharp change in the way Canadians pay for buying mutual funds. Today, the most popular way is to commit to paying a redemption fee when the fund shares eventually are sold. This type of charge, known as a back-end load, or a deferred sales charge, seems to appeal to people's natural tendency to want to buy now and pay later. Often these deferred charges diminish gradually over a period of time, usually six years, until they disappear altogether. It is worth noting, however, that if the fund has met your expectations and increased in value, the charge will be levied on a larger amount than the amount of your initial investment.

Many fund companies today give the customer the choice between a front-end and a back-end load. The so-called optional load fund, which has become popular, allows the client to go either way. Choosing between a front-end-load, back-end-load or no-load mutual fund isn't as simple as it seems. Although it might be tempting to defer a sales charge to a later year, or even to pay no sales charge at all, these types of funds have other ways of recouping their costs of distribution. Annual fees, which are deducted from the fund's net asset value, tend to be higher in deferred-load and no-load funds than in funds that levy a sales charge up front.

Once you own shares in a mutual fund, the most prominent fee you encounter is the management fee, which mainly goes toward compensating the fund manager for services. Equity funds generally have higher management fees than bond funds because they require more time and market research to administer. Fees vary widely, although the typical Canadian equity fund has a management fee of about 1.5% to 2% of the fund's assets. On top of this, mutual fund companies normally tack on another fee of 0.25% to 0.50% to cover other services, such as distribution costs. Added together, these fees are known as the fund expense ratio, details of which are contained in the individual fund's prospectus.

What do these fees mean to the investor? They could mean a lot. Before you get anything back from your mutual fund investment, the fund company each year skims off as much as 2.5%, in the example given here, of the fund's total assets. This might not seem much when markets are rapidly rising. But in a year when markets are flat or down, management still takes its fees.

With all these charges, wouldn't it be cheaper, then, to just buy stocks directly?

In fact, buying mutual funds is frequently more expensive than buying equity securities, even after factoring in commissions on buying and later selling the stocks. But it's important to remember that mutual fund shares are not ordinary securities. In effect they are a service contract entitling you to a unique package of securities and services not available with straight bond or stock purchases. These services include continuing professional management, diversification, ease of purchase and redemption, liquidity and a pro-rata ownership in the fund's net assets.

Besides mutual funds, are there other ways for ordinary investors to have their money managed professionally?

Closed-end Funds

So far we've talked only about mutual funds, or open-end investment funds, which are the most popular form of managed investments. There is another class of fund known as the closed-end investment fund, so called because the number of its shares or units outstanding remains relatively fixed.

Shares of closed-end investment companies are offered to investors at the time the fund is set up. Proceeds from this sale of equity are then invested in a diversified portfolio that is readjusted depending on market conditions. As with a mutual fund, a closed-end fund places its shareholders' money into investments that reflect the fund's particular policies and objectives. A closed-end fund is allowed to raise additional capital by issuing debt securities. However, additional offerings of the fund's equity are either infrequent or not permitted by its charter, and the common stock is not redeemed except in unusual circumstances, such as a tender offer, or when the fund is wound up.

A list of closed-end funds and their net asset values appears in some of the weekend papers.

There are about 40 closed-end funds in Canada. Unlike a mutual fund, whose shares are issued and redeemed by the fund itself, shares of closed-end funds trade on stock exchanges or on the over-the-counter market. Thus, when you buy shares in a closed-end fund, unless you're buying at the initial public offering, the purchase price goes to the seller of the stock, and doesn't contribute to the fund's own assets.

The market price of closed-end fund shares typically is at a large discount to the fund's net asset value. This discount reflects the market's view that the closed-end fund is a going concern that is unlikely to be wound up and its paper assets realized at their then current break-up value.

Wrap Accounts

Another type of managed investment account, aimed at investors with a larger amount of capital, is the so-called wrap account. These accounts, which are sponsored by brokerage firms, were introduced to Canada in the last two years after becoming popular in the United States.

Brokerage firms traditionally run non-discretionary accounts, which means the broker needs to obtain the client's permission to buy or sell securities, and the client pays a charge for each transaction. In a wrap account, which also is known as a wrap fee program, the client pays a single fee based on a percentage of assets invested. The investment is then turned over to a professional money manager on a fully discretionary basis, which means investment decisions are left up to the money manager. Brokerage firms attempt to customize a wrap account to the client's investment objectives and risk tolerance when the account is first opened, and subsequently at regular intervals. Although each wrap account is managed separately from other wrap accounts at the same brokerage firm, it is kept consistent with a model portfolio suitable to other clients with similar objectives.

There are a number of variations on the wrap account. For one thing, some brokerage firms employ their own money managers to run the accounts. Others claim they attract better talent by contracting with independent managers.

What kind of charges would I expect to pay?

One firm requires a minimum investment of $150,000 for an equity wrap account ($250,000 for a balanced or bond portfolio), and charges an annual fee of 2.75% of the assets invested. The fee declines as the investment grows in size. At another dealer the minimum investment is $50,000, and the annual fee is 2.5%. Judging by the U.S. experience with wrap accounts, we can expect the minimum investment levels to decline as competition for business picks up.

How much would I need to invest before getting more personalized service – say, my own investment counsellor?

You'd probably need at least $1 million of investments to catch the ear of an established money manager, although half a million might be enough if a manager were looking to drum up business. With this money you would open a discretionary account.

Sometimes an ordinary Investment Advisor can act as a discretionary money manager for a client, but usually just for short periods of time, such as when the client is away on vacation. However, the IA is prohibited from soliciting such business, and generally must clear all discretionary transactions with a director of the firm. When an IA does solicit discretionary business from a client, he does so on behalf of the firm's money management department. Such accounts often are referred to as managed accounts.

Discretionary account: the money manager can buy and sell securities in the portfolio without obtaining the clients' permission for each transaction.

I know you don't get something for nothing, but these management fees could take a big chunk out of your investment capital! I could live with that if the returns were good, but what if they were charging me a fee and losing money? I don't think I could handle that.

By the time this course is finished, there'll be no reason why you should have to. You'll be able to make your own intelligent investment decisions in conjunction with an IA. Next week we'll show you how to choose one. See you then.

Summary

There are a number of ways that you can make use of the talents of professional money managers. Buying mutual funds is one of them.

A mutual fund uses the money invested in it to buy a portfolio of securities. By owning units of a mutual fund, investors acquire a piece of that portfolio. Units are sold by the fund at that day's net asset value, plus any applicable sales charge. Investors wanting to dispose of their units sell them back to the fund, again at that day's net asset value. Whether you buy your units through an investment dealer or from a fund's own sales representative, you are buying new units from the fund rather than existing units from a selling investor.

Many people associate mutual funds with equities. This is only sometimes the case. There are many types of funds, each with its own investment objectives: bond, money market, balanced, equity, and global funds, to name a few, each invest in particular asset classes. As well, fund managers employ differing types of investing styles. So even though buying a mutual fund means you are buying professional management, it still requires some investment knowledge to choose the fund that best matches your requirements.

There are a number of fees associated with mutual fund ownership. Besides the sales charge, which can be paid either at the time of purchase or when the units are sold, investors pay a management fee which is deducted from the fund's assets. Some funds collect other fees such as distribution fees, which are also deducted from the fund's assets. The total of all these fees is known as the fund's management expense ratio, and is expressed as a percent of its assets.

Mutual funds are also known as open-end funds because they are always issuing new units and redeeming existing ones from investors. A closed-end investment fund, on the other hand, has a fixed number of shares. Although it too uses the money it raises to invest in a portfolio of securities, it differs from a mutual fund in that its shares trade on a stock exchange, much like the shares of the companies in which it invests.

Many investment dealers offer wrap accounts. Investors pay a percentage of assets to have their money managed by a professional. Some firms hire their own manager to look after these accounts, while others contract the work out to independent managers.

Chapter 7
Getting Into the Market

Become an experienced investor with the help of the right IA.

Good evening, everybody. Tonight's seminar is going to be a little different than our previous sessions. In the last few meetings, you've had to grapple with some pretty difficult theoretical concepts about investing – such as what securities are and how the securities system works. Tonight we get to relax a bit and talk about putting some of that theory into practice.

First of all, I'll outline the basic steps you should follow when you're getting into the market for the first time. Then I'll talk about the things you should continue to do as long as you remain in the market. You're going to find that I refer a lot to other sessions. So feel free to look back if you need to refresh your memory on certain topics. After all, investing isn't a closed book exam – you get to peek as much as you like!

First Steps *Take Stock of Yourself*

The first step towards getting into the market is taking stock of yourself. Everyone in this classroom is different, and there's no way I can set out one way of investing that's going to be right for all of you. Pat, you've said that you're a conservative person who's here to learn enough to invest intelligently with guidance from your IA. Jason, on the other hand, seems to me to be a bit of a risk-taker, and a go-it-alone kind of investor. No offence taken, I hope, Jason.

There's room for both of you in the securities markets. But you have to think carefully about which type of investor you want to be, and what kind of investing you want to do. And you should think about this **before** you get started. Someone once said that the market can be an expensive place to find out who you are.

For starters, you should ask yourself the classic financial planning questions. We're going to cover these in more detail in our next session. But just to give you a flavour of what I'm talking about, here are some of the questions you need to answer before you begin investing.

How much money do you have to invest? What's your time horizon for investing? And what are your goals for the money?

Now when I say goals, I mean something more specific than saying that you want to become a millionaire. For example, is safety of principal the most important thing to you? Or do you need to be able to get the money out quickly if you need it – that is, do you need a very liquid investment? Are you trying to increase the principal you're investing – in other words, make a capital gain? Or are you looking for steady income? Then again, maybe you'd like the best of all worlds and get a little of all of those things?

These questions deal with your financial situation and goals. They might sound complicated, but you should be able to come up with some straightforward, black-and-white answers with a little work. You can do this on your own with the aid of financial planning books or some of the forms I'll hand out next class, or you might want to consult a broker or financial advisor. We'll talk about this more in a minute.

There are other questions you need to answer that require a little soul-searching. Such as, how much of a risk-taker are you? You can think of risk tolerance as a spectrum ranging from conservative to speculative, with varying shades in between. Pat might be at the conservative side of the spectrum, for example, and Jason at the other side. Where you lie in the spectrum will help determine the degree of safety that you should aim for when investing.

But don't think of risk tolerance as just a personality quirk. It also depends on your financial and personal situation. Maybe for fun you like to skydive, ride fast motorcycles and bike to work in downtown Toronto. But if you have limited financial resources, no pension plan and three children headed for college, it may not be a good idea to take a lot of risks with your savings. And maybe you should think about taking out some heavy-duty life insurance – or stop skydiving and take up needlepoint.

Another set of important questions has to do with the process of investing itself. What's your level of investment knowledge? And how much time do you want to spend thinking about your finances? I assume since you're all taking this course that you have some interest in financial matters, and you're eager to learn. But even if you're all fired up about investing at the moment, think carefully about how much time and effort you're going to be willing to spend in the future. Will you want to take the time needed to be an active, educated, self-directed investor? Or will you want some assistance in making financial decisions?

That brings us to the next step in beginning to invest – choosing an Investment Advisor.

Choose an Investment Advisor

In our earlier session on how the securities system works, we talked about the role of brokers and investment dealers. As I mentioned then, the terms broker and dealer can be somewhat confusing. Technically, they are different. A broker acts as an agent, buying and selling an investment on behalf of the client, and receiving a commission for the service. In contrast, a dealer buys an investment product with its own money and resells the product to customers.

Another difference is that traditionally a broker or brokerage house tended to specialize in stocks, while an investment dealer focused on bonds. But today most investment firms trade both stocks and bonds, and can be referred to as either brokers or investment dealers.

Just to add to the confusion, the term broker is sometimes used to refer to both the investment firm – that is, the brokerage house – and to the people employed by the brokerage house to deal with clients. And guess what – these people also can be referred to by other names, such as Investment Advisor, Account Representative, Investment Salesperson or Registered Representative. In our discussion, I'm going to refer to the person with whom you deal at an investment house as an Investment Advisor – commonly called an IA.

The requirements to become an IA in Canada are some of the most stringent in the world. An IA must be registered with the provincial securities commission to sell securities. Before you can be registered, you must pass the Canadian Securities Course, and an exam based on the Conduct and Practices Handbook, offered by the Canadian Securities Institute. As a new IA you must undergo a 90-day training program provided by your company. During those three months, you're barred from dealing with clients. After that you're supervised very closely and have to complete a demanding one-year financial planning course to keep your license. Other qualifications may be required depending on the role that the IA performs, who they work for, and the products they sell. For example, to buy and sell options on behalf of clients, an IA must pass the Options course offered by the Institute.

Now that we have a handle on what IAs are, let's talk about what they can do for you. IAs have two levels of responsibility. Their basic role is to trade securities on behalf of clients. When you want to buy stocks or bonds, you call your broker and place the order. In general, the broker relays the order to the firm's trading desk – the trade takes place – and the broker takes care of any necessary paperwork. This includes sending you a confirmation of the trade, and updating your account. The firm also clears and settles the trade. That means making sure that you pay for the securities you buy, and that the person who sold them to you delivers the securities to your account.

Those are the essential order execution services provided by all investment houses. In addition, an IA working for a full-service firm will provide you with investment research and advice. Other brokerages choose not to provide clients with advice, and only execute clients' orders. These are called "discount" brokers, because they often charge lower commission fees than full-service brokers.

So when you start looking for an IA, the first thing you have to do is decide whether you want to use a full-service or discount firm. A discount broker is a good choice if you are a knowledgeable, experienced investor who knows exactly which financial products you want to buy and you have the time to devote to managing your investments.

If you are interested in having assistance in making investment choices, however, a full-service firm may be for you.

Once you've made the decision about which kind of firm you want, you can begin your search. It's a good idea to choose a firm that's a member of one of Canada's Self-Regulatory Organizations (SROs) – the stock exchanges or the Investment Dealers Association of Canada (IDA). You can obtain lists of member firms from the exchanges or the IDA, or you can look in the telephone book. The SROs have minimum standards of conduct for their members, and jointly operate important industry organizations like the Canadian Securities Institute. The CSI not only educates the public, it also sets educational standards for brokers and others who operate within the SRO system.

Another key organization is the Canadian Investor Protection Fund. The Fund protects clients in case a member firm goes under. If you have a general account with a brokerage house that's a member of an exchange or the IDA, your account is protected for up to $500,000 in cash and securities, with a $60,000 cash limit. You'll probably sleep better at night knowing that you don't have to worry about the financial health of the brokerage firm that's investing your money.

Next, I'd suggest calling a few firms before making your choice. Ask them if they are interested in your account. Ask about their commissions and fees. And if you're interested in a full-service firm, ask the branch or sales manager to recommend one or two brokers at the firm who would be good choices to handle your account. Then interview them. Your broker will have a big impact on your finances, so take the time to get to know him or her and decide whether this is the person for you.

I've been talking at you for a while now. Let's take a moment to stretch, and I'll be happy to answer questions about anything I've said up to this point.

 As you said earlier, Enzo, I'm the kind of investor who wants to have help from a financial advisor. What should I look for when I'm interviewing potential IAs?

I'd start off with asking about their education and experience. The CSI has an advanced course, for example, called Canadian Investment Management. It deals with advanced wealth management techniques and portfolio management. If the broker has taken it, that indicates a certain level of experience and knowledge that could be useful if you're looking for help with making sound investment choices. Some of the most experienced IAs have the letters FCSI after their names. This stands for Fellow of the Canadian Securities Institute, and means the IA is somebody who has an exemplary track-record and has met stringent educational requirements. Also ask what the IA's typical client is like. Say you're a senior citizen – yes, Pat, I know you're a long way off. But if you were a senior on a fixed income, you'd have special needs, and it might be reassuring to know that your broker has other clients like you. Some brokers may even specialize in meeting the needs of seniors, or of other segments of the investing public.

It's worthwhile to talk about mutual expectations, too. Discuss the services you're looking for, such as how frequently you want to be in contact. If you're not a very active investor, it may be unrealistic to expect your advisor to call you constantly with research and recommendations – and in fact, you probably would prefer that they didn't. But to make sure you're on the same wavelength, talk about it first.

But it's not just a matter of expectations, is it? Isn't there a certain standard of service I'm entitled to?

Absolutely. There are numerous rules and regulations that advisors must follow. Most important is the cardinal rule guiding their behaviour – Know Your Client. Know Your Client means that the key focus of IAs must be suitability of investments. The IA must make a concerted effort to understand the client's financial and personal status and goals and only make recommendations that reflect these criteria.

Let me read you a passage from the CSI's Conduct and Practices Handbook for Securities Industry Professionals. It says:

every member shall use due diligence:

> *to learn the essential facts relative to every client and to every order or account accepted;*

> *to ensure that the acceptance of any order for any account is within the bounds of good business practice; and*

> *to ensure that recommendations made for any account are appropriate for the client and in keeping with his or her investment objectives.*

This is the bottom-line behaviour for an IA – what at the very minimum you should expect from your financial advisor.

As an investor, you too should make suitability your main focus. As we discussed earlier, before you start investing, you should consider your financial situation and your financial goals and think about the kind of investment products that would suit you. Then, when you're choosing an advisor, discuss your views on what you think are suitable investments. You and your IA should see eye-to-eye on your needs.

Open an Account

So let's say you've found an IA who has the experience and knowledge to help you make suitable decisions. How does this very important person find out what is suitable for you?

The main tool for IAs is the New Client Application Form – the form you fill out when you first open an account with a brokerage firm. It is here that you must crystallize your financial objectives. This form provides the key information that will help your advisor choose suitable investments for you. It's in your best interest to make sure every fact on this application is as accurate and complete as you can make it.

The NCAF asks you a lot of questions, such as:

- Your full name
- Your permanent address, home and business telephone numbers
- Citizenship
- Occupation, employer, type of business
- If you are an officer, director or in a control position of a public company
- Age
- Investment objectives – risk tolerance
- Investment knowledge
- Net worth and earnings
- Bank and credit reference

Some of the questions may seem nosy – like your occupation or whether you're married. But this can be important in unexpected ways. For example, your occupation may indicate your level of understanding of the securities business. And, in addition, who your employer is could be relevant to guard against insider trading.

So don't be shy about telling your advisor the answers to these questions. At the same time, don't exaggerate facts, such as your income or level of investment knowledge or willingness to tolerate risk. If you do so, your IA might start recommending inappropriate investments. And that could get you into trouble.

Your advisor will also ask you what type of account you want to open. The two main types of accounts are cash and margin.

If you open a regular cash account, you must make full payment for purchases or full delivery for sales on or before the settlement date. The settlement date for most securities is three business days after the trade.

On the other hand, if you open a margin account you will be able to buy securities on credit. You'll pay only part of the full price at the time when you make a trade. The part you pay, by the way, is called the margin. The brokerage firm will lend you the remainder, charging you interest on the loan.

Buying securities on margin can be a good deal, and if you are an experienced investor you might want to explore this option. But there are pitfalls. When a brokerage firm lends you the money to buy securities, it uses the securities in your account as collateral. If those securities drop in price, the company may require you to advance more money. This is known as a margin call – and answering the call isn't optional. If you don't advance the money in time, the securities may be sold, possibly at a loss to you, in order to settle the account. So don't use margin unless you'll be able to come up with the cash to answer any margin call quickly and easily.

Whichever type of account you open, it's a good idea to talk with your broker about what your responsibilities are under the terms of the account. Some of these are spelled out in a document known as a Client's Agreement, which will be sent to you when you open an account. For example, many agreements for both cash and margin accounts specify that the firm has the right to close out the account if proper settlement isn't made. Let's say you fail to pay in time for securities that you asked your advisor to buy. Under most agreements, the firm would legally be able to sell securities in your account to pay the outstanding balance. It's your responsibility to live up to the terms of the agreement.

One more thing – when you open an account with a firm, open a file of your own at home. Keep copies of every document that's important to you as an investor – your New Client Application Form, the Client's Agreement, and any statements sent by your advisor. It's a good way to keep on top of your investments. And if you ever have any problems, having the documents handy will help you find a solution much faster.

An Ongoing Journey

Opening an account is just the first step. Now you start the real business of being an investor – and that's investing, of course!

Decide on Investments

First you have to decide what you want to buy. If you've done your financial planning homework, you should already know the types of investment that are suited to your needs. Now you have to narrow in on a specific investment. To do so, consult the many sources of information available to investors. These range from mass media like newspapers to detailed documents like annual reports and prospectuses. Then analyse the securities that interest you, using the techniques we discussed in our third and fourth sessions. There are many other books and courses that also teach methods to evaluate securities.

If you are dealing with a full-service investment house, you should ask your IA for research and recommendations. But don't feel obliged to act on all recommendations. Your broker has a responsibility to recommend investments that are suited to your needs. The final decision, however, is always up to you. Don't make an investment that you don't understand or that you don't agree with. Do your own thinking. If your broker is making recommendations that don't suit you, tell him or her how you feel. It's possible that your advisor hasn't understood your needs properly or that he or she has a different view on what's right for you. But if you've discussed the issue and you continue to disagree with recommendations, consider looking for another advisor.

Initiate the Trade

Once you've made an investment decision, it's time to put the trade into action. Let's say you want to buy a security. You call your broker and discuss the trade. There are four main pieces of information you'll need to specify: the name of the security; whether you want to buy or sell it; the quantity you want to trade; and the type of order. The first two things are easy to convey to your broker. To identify a bond, you specify the issuer, the coupon and the maturity. For example, you might say that you want to buy the Government of Canada bond with a coupon of 9–%, maturing in the year 2021.

To identify a stock, state the name of the issuer, and any specific details about the issue. Companies can issue more than one type of stock. For example, the Bank of Nova Scotia has both common and preferred issues. So be sure to tell your advisor exactly which one you want.

The Quantity

In addition, when you are trading a security, you should be aware that there are traditional ways to express quantities. If you are buying stocks, often the number of shares in an order is expressed as a "board lot." A board lot is a trading unit composed of a set number of shares. The number of shares in a board lot depends on the price. For stocks priced at and above $1, for instance, a board lot is composed of 100 shares. So if you want to buy 1,000 shares of ACME and it's trading at $5, you would tell your broker that you want to buy 10 board lots. On the other hand, for stocks that trade at under 10 cents on the Montreal, Toronto and Alberta Stock Exchanges, a board lot is made up of 1,000 shares.

A number of shares that is less than a board lot – say 50 shares of ACME – is referred to as an "odd lot". And a number of shares that can be expressed as a board lot and an odd lot – such as 450 shares – is known as a mixed lot.

Before you start trading, ask your broker to explain the terminology they use to express quantities of securities. And when you're giving an order, make sure there's no confusion about exactly how much you want. You don't want to end up with 1,000 shares of a stock when you really wanted 100 – or vice versa!

For bonds, the quantity is generally expressed in terms of the face value of the bond. If you've ever bought Canada Savings Bonds, you're probably familiar with this idea. For example, you might have bought one $1,000 CSB, and five $100 CSBs. It's the same with other bonds. A big investor, for instance, might buy a $100,000 Government of Canada bond with a 9–% coupon, maturing in 2021.

And if the price was, say 101.50, he would pay $101,500.

Types of Orders

That's right, Jason. Another part of your order you should think about is its type. The type of order can indicate several things, such as the price at which the trade will take place; and the time limit on the trade.

Market

In terms of price, the two main types of orders are market and limit orders. If you place a market order for a security, you will pay, if you're buying, or receive, if you're selling, the best price available at the time. An order that doesn't specify a price will usually be considered a market order.

Limit

If you place a limit order, you actually specify the price at which you are willing to trade the security. For instance, if you want to buy a security, you might set a price of $8 per share that you're willing to pay. Your order will only be executed if the market for that stock moves to that price or a better one.

Day

In terms of time, the two main types of orders are day and open orders. A day order is an order to buy or sell that is valid only for the day it is given. Say you tell your IA you want to buy 100 shares of ACME at a limit price of $8. The order can only be filled if the market price for ACME moves to $8 or better. If the order isn't filled by the end of the day, the order will be cancelled. It's important to note that all orders are considered to be day orders unless you tell your broker otherwise.

Open or Good Till Cancelled

An open order is also known as a Good Till Cancelled order. As the name suggests, this means your order will remain on the broker's books until its is executed or cancelled. However, many firms will limit an open order to a set amount of time – perhaps one month – and then remind clients about it. That way customers don't forget about an old order and then become surprised when it is suddenly executed.

Good Through Date

A customer can also specify a Good Through Date order. This is an order to buy or sell that is valid for a time period specified by the client. As an example, you could give a limit order for ACME that is Good Through April 27. If it hasn't been filled by that time, the order is cancelled.

Any Part

There are many other types of orders that indicate the way a client wants a particular order handled. In general, an order will be considered an Any Part order. That means that if you've given an order for 100 shares of ACME at $8, but only 50 shares becomes available at that price, you will end up buying those 50 shares.

All or None

However, you could specify that your order is an All or None order. Your order would have to be filled in its entirety on one day, or not filled at all. So if only 50 shares are available, your order would not be executed.

Fill or Kill

A Fill or Kill order states that as soon as part of the order is filled, the remainder is cancelled. If you want 500 shares of ACME, for instance, and only 100 are available at present, you would obtain those 100 shares, but the order for the remaining 400 would be cancelled.

Change Former Order

A type of order that could be important to you is the Cancel or Change Former Order. Always remember that if you've placed an order and it hasn't been filled either partially or totally yet, you have the right to cancel it or change it.

Just to round off our discussion of types of orders, here are a few more.

Either/Or

An Either/Or order means that the client puts in an order to buy or sell one security while another order or orders for other securities are waiting to be executed. As soon as one order is executed, the other is cancelled. Either one or the other is executed, but not both.

Contingent

A Contingent order is an order to buy one security and simultaneously to sell another security. For example, you might place a contingent order to sell 100 shares of ACME, and buy 100 shares of Zebra Corp. Contingent orders for two securities can be entered: a) at the market; b) at the same price; c) at a certain point spread; d) with a share ratio (e.g. 100 shares of ACME and 200 shares of Zebra). One side of the transaction cannot be completed without the other.

Switch

A Switch order is similar but not identical. It usually involves selling one security, and then using the proceeds to buy another.

Stop Loss

Another interesting type of order is known as a Stop Loss. This is an order to sell which becomes effective as a market order when the price of a board lot of stock declines to or below the stated limit or stop price. For example, if you bought Zebra shares at $10, you might decide to protect yourself by placing a stop loss order at $8. If Zebra shares declined to or below $8, your shares would be sold. Hopefully your loss would be limited to about $2 a share. However, there's no guarantee of this, since your sell order would go into the market as a market order – meaning you'd try to get the best price possible at the time. That might be $8, or if the stock continued to decline, it might be less than $8.

I know I've covered a lot of ground here. Are there any questions?

I've taken down all these types of orders, but isn't there one other important type of order you should talk about, Enzo? I'm interested in learning about short sales.

Short Selling

I guess I shouldn't be surprised that a technique like short selling would appeal to you, Jason. Short selling can be profitable. But it can also be dangerous.

A short sale occurs when you place an order to sell a security that you don't own. Your broker would borrow the shares for you from the firm's inventory or from another client. You might short sell if you believed that the price of the stock was going to fall, and you would be able to cover the sale by buying back the stock later at a lower price. For example, you might short sell ACME when it's trading at $8, and then buy it in the market when it's at $6. You would make a $2 per share profit. However, if the price of ACME had gone up, you would have lost money.

Just as with a regular transaction, you would have bought shares and sold shares, and your profit or loss would be the difference between the buy and sell prices. As usual, you would be trying to buy low and sell high – but with short selling, the "sell high" comes before the "buy low".

The danger with short selling comes with the potential for loss. If you had bought a board lot of ACME at $8, what's the most you could lose?

I can tell you that! You'd lose your $800 investment if the stock went to 0.

That's right. The most you could lose is the money you invested. But that's not the case with short selling. If you shorted a board lot of ACME at $8, the most money you could lose if things didn't go your way is impossible to determine in advance, because we don't know how high ACME could go.

If I shorted ACME it would go to at least $50.

And if you bought it back at $50, you would lose $4,200 – the $5,000 you would pay to buy it less the $800 you sold it for. This far exceeds the amount you invested, which in this case would be the 50% margin requirement – $400 to start with and more as the stock climbed.

But why would Jason buy the stock back at $50? Why not wait 'til it fell back down?

*Because **my** personal investing technique seems to be buy high and sell low!*

In fact, Pat, Jason would not have to buy in at $50. If he could meet the margin requirement and if he was patient, he might be able to wait out the upward move, although there would be no guarantee that ACME would go back down to $8. But there is no time limit on short selling.

Some of you look a little confused by my explanation, and that's not surprising. Short selling is a specialized technique that should be used only by very knowledgeable and experienced investors. It's also something you must discuss thoroughly with your broker before doing. That's not just a suggestion. It is actually illegal for a seller not to declare that he or she is selling short at the time of placing the order.

Okay, let's step back from the complicated world of special types of orders and pretend we're placing a run-of-the-mill order. Let's say you want to buy 10 board lots of Zebra Corp. You tell your broker the name of the company, the quantity, and the fact that you are willing to pay whatever price is going in the market. In other words, you're placing a market order.

If Zebra is an actively traded stock, your order may actually be executed within seconds, and your broker will confirm this over the phone. You will also be sent a written confirmation.

Settle Your Account

The written confirmation will summarize the details of the trade, such as the quantity and the exact unit price at which the securities were traded. You should check to make sure that the order was executed as you instructed, and that the information shown is correct.

The investment firm's commission will also be listed. In the 1980s, a system of negotiated commissions was introduced in the Canadian stock exchanges, replacing the previous fixed schedule. You can shop around for the best rates. In general, IAs charge a percentage of the value of the order, depending on the order's size. There is a minimum fee, so the commission on very small orders may seem comparatively large.

The written confirmation will also state the total amount that you owe the firm, if you bought stocks or bonds, or that the firm owes you, if you sold securities. As we talked about earlier, if you have a regular cash account with your investment firm, you must make full payment for purchases or full delivery for sales on or before the settlement date. For most securities, the settlement date is three business days after the day of the trade. There are some differences, however; for example, bonds issued or guaranteed by the Government of Canada with a term of less than three years have two days to settle; and Government of Canada treasury bills settle the same day as the transaction. The settlement date is generally listed on the written confirmation. As we noted earlier, it is very important that you settle your account within the set settlement period.

Monitor Your Investments

Once you've settled your first trade, you're officially a securities investor. Then the process starts all over again as you work to diversify your portfolio of investments.

Even if you're not actively accumulating more securities, you still have work to do as an investor. As long as you are invested in the capital markets, you must do several things: monitor your account; monitor your portfolio; and monitor your financial situation.

Monitoring your account shouldn't be too difficult. In addition to sending you written confirmation every time you make a trade, your IA must send you monthly statements detailing the activity in your account. If there is no activity in a month, no statement will be sent. You will receive quarterly statements, however, as long as you have cash or securities in your account.

Be sure to read over every statement, even if you haven't been trading recently. If you don't understand what your statement shows, ask your advisor or another knowledgeable person to explain it to you. And if you ever see something in your account you don't agree with – say a trade you didn't authorize or another error – report it in writing immediately. If it's not corrected on your next statement, write to your IA and his or her supervisor again to tell them of the error. Most statements note that any discrepancies must be reported within a certain time frame, so it's very important to address any problems immediately. Remember to keep copies of your statements and of every letter you send in your own financial file – the one I made you open a few minutes ago.

 What if writing letters doesn't solve the problem? Or what if there's no written record to go back to? What should I do?

Most problems can be solved within the branch. Should it be necessary, you can contact the Investment Dealers Association; assuming, of course, that your account is at a member firm. The IDA can investigate your situation and get to the bottom of it. They can require a member to submit background information or attend a hearing. Problems in the industry don't usually have to go this far to get resolved, but it's good to know that the process is there if you need it.

In addition to monitoring your account, monitor the securities that make up your portfolio. You already know that you should do a reasonable amount of research and thinking before you buy a security. And you shouldn't stop once the trade is made. The company in which you invested may change, or the economic situation may change. Periodically review each security to make sure it's right for you.

Of course, to do this properly you also have to monitor your own financial situation. Your own status and goals may change in a way that makes a security no longer suitable for you. And if circumstances do change, don't just keep it to yourself. Remember to tell your IA. If you should experience a big change in your net worth or annual income, for example – hopefully for the better – tell your investment firm. Your IA bases his or her recommendations on the facts known about you. So make sure they're right.

Finally, monitor the securities business and the capital markets. What you've learned in this seminar tonight is a good starting place. But there's plenty more to know. Keep learning through this course and others, and through books. Continued learning about the market is the best investment you'll ever make.

See you all next week.

Summary

The first step in getting into the market is to do some self examination. Try to quantify your time horizon, the amount of money you have available, the level of risk you can live with, and your investment objectives.

Then you should choose an investment dealer and an IA. This is an important decision, so talk to a few candidates before deciding. You then fill out the New Client Application Form and open an account. A margin account lets you borrow part of the cost of the securities you purchase, whereas with a cash account you are expected to pay for your purchases in full.

You then must decide what to buy. Your IA will make suggestions and provide you with research reports, but you make the final decision. The IA will also advise you on how much to buy and what type of order to use. Experienced investors who think that a stock is going to decline in value can execute a short sale, which will be profitable for them if the stock does decline.

After paying for the transaction, your next task is to monitor your account and your investments. Check the accuracy of the statements the investment dealer sends you. Regularly review the prospects of the companies you have invested in. Review your own financial position, and notify your IA of any changes. Finally, keep learning about the investment markets.

Chapter 8
Financial Planning

Putting your investment knowledge to work.

We've touched on just about every aspect of investing. How do we fit all of this information together now? And how do we know if we are on the right track or not?

The best place to start is at the beginning – that is, drawing up your financial plan. You must set your own goals and objectives and prepare a budget. Once you have these basics decided, you can begin the investment process. Many people start out by investing first and then devise a plan. That's putting the cart before the horse. Know where you are going before you start the trip.

That's simple – everyone wants to be rich. That's why lottery tickets sell so well.

Sometimes I think lottery tickets sell simply because most people have failed at their financial planning. A lottery ticket or at least the dream of winning is the ultimate quick fix. "If only I could win $10,000 or $100,000 or $1,000,000, I wouldn't have any more financial problems." While occasionally the dream of winning a lottery can be a pleasant diversion, it's not the kind of financial planning most of us can afford. Financial independence does not occur by luck but rather by choice.

And I really don't want to be rich. I would like to be comfortable, to be able to pay for my children's schooling and to retire in comfort. I don't want to have to worry about having too little or even too much.

I don't think I could ever have too much money.

While your objectives may be different, the planning that you do now to reach your personal goals can be similar. Obviously, Jason is willing to take on more risk, so his strategy or actual investments will be different from those of a more conservative investor like Pat. But developing a financial plan is pretty much the same from one person to another. And if you don't start, you won't finish.

The Financial Plan

To start the process, you must realize that a good plan 1) must be do-able, 2) can accommodate the bumps and grinds of daily life, 3) is not intimidating and 4) can provide for life's necessities as well as some luxuries. It will, by design, be a personal and unique strategy for you and your family. This will not be an easy process, as there are important decisions to be made along the way.

The first thing you must do when starting to construct a financial plan is to record your current situation. We're providing some sample forms you can use for this purpose. First, you should fill out a Financial Information form. List all financial institutions you deal with: investment dealers, financial planners, mutual fund companies, banks, trusts, and credit unions as well as insurance agents. Account numbers and contact people should be listed clearly; you may not be around to explain things to someone else. The name and contact information for your lawyer, accountant and doctor should also be recorded. This may be used by either your family or your executor. Make it clear and concise. List the location of all important papers including passports, previous years' tax returns, wills, insurance policies, mortgage documentation, property deeds, and loans and IOUs. List the location of your safety deposit box and its keys. But most importantly, tell someone, such as your spouse, that you have made this list, and where to find it.

Sample forms are at the back of this chapter

Next, prepare a statement of your current net worth. This is really just a simple balance sheet that will concisely show you how much money you have, or don't have, as the case may be. It is a snapshot picture really, valid only on the day it is calculated; but you have to have a starting point so as to be able to measure how well you are doing when it comes time for review.

Now comes the income statement. Once you have calculated your income, calculate your expenses and see what is left over. This balance is what you can invest. If the amount is not significant, try reworking your budget to see if you can increase the investment component. Once you reach what you think is the maximum amount, consider the investment spectrum. We'll get to it later.

You're assuming that we have all the necessary information at our fingertips. What's the best way to keep track of it all?

I'm going to use my computer to take care of all my financial dealings – I can enter all the information from my bank account as well as my investment accounts, then chart my progress.

Do all investors have to use such complicated methods? One – I don't have a computer and two – I don't have time to keep such detailed records. I just use a shoe box now for tax receipts and the like.

Some people will want to use a computer-based system to keep track of their investments and budget. This is appropriate if you are computer literate and, of course, if you have a computer. There are some excellent financial software products available, some for well under $100. Whatever system you choose, think about it carefully. Will you consistently maintain your computer-based records or is such a system more trouble than it's worth? For myself, I use a very simple record book – I like the simple approach.

The Life Cycle

Once you know where you are financially, you can look toward developing a plan. It can be useful to start with an overview of the five stages of an adult's financial life, see where you fit in, and have some concept of what lies ahead.

Phase One – Starting Out

This first phase begins after the college or university years. Most people start their first job and move into their first apartment. It is the beginning of a career and could entail a lot of capital expenditure on those mundane household things. There are few responsibilities; it's a time of testing your wings and learning. Cash inflow is meagre while cash outflow is usually very large. This is an easy time to get into financial trouble through overspending. A key word at this stage could be "Budget".

Investment-wise – while it may be difficult at this stage to save, a portion of income should be set aside, if only to introduce discipline into your life. Big purchases should not be made on credit. In terms of investments, Guaranteed Investment Certificates may be too boring, while option and commodity trading may have more appeal. This is a time for adventure, and speculative trading fits in with this adventuresome spirit. Risks should not be open ended though and should be limited to an affordable amount. That means no short selling. But while emotionally you may be ready and willing to speculate, there is usually one small problem – lack of funds. A savings plan could be used to accumulate funds for risky investments. At this point in one's life a high risk security could be attractive if only from a learning point of view. It is probably the most appropriate time for such speculative trading because losses will not affect retirement planning drastically at this point in time. As well, any losses that do occur with speculative trading will have a sobering influence on the young investor.

I'm surprised you're suggesting speculative investments for young people who are just starting out. Shouldn't you learn to walk before you start to run?

Absolutely. I'm not recommending that people start their investing lives by going on a speculative binge. It does make more sense to start slowly. As you gain experience and knowledge, you can move on to more complex and speculative investments. You could even conceive of a knowledge cycle that works differently than the life cycle: you start out at the conservative end of the investment spectrum. As you acquire more knowledge and, not incidentally, more assets, you begin to branch out and take on more risk. You work toward a diversified portfolio with a mix of investment products and risk levels.

But you have to ask yourself: is that how we really behave? It's also true that we tend to be more aggressive and daring when we are young, and we gravitate toward less extreme positions as we get older. I'm a much more conservative investor now than I was ten years ago, although others may not be – no generalization works for everybody. I mentioned speculative investments in Phase One to acknowledge this natural tendency toward the extreme. If you're at this stage and you're attracted to risk, go ahead. Just try to learn as much as you can about your chosen investment.

Maybe I missed out on this investing stage – I was using all my funds to set up my business. But how would you set up a savings plan at this point?

Common wisdom would say "Pay yourself first". That means that out of every paycheque, including bonuses and commissions, if you are lucky enough to be paid in this manner, comes a certain dollar amount or percentage. This is not easy when your income is low and there are so many things you may need or want, so many things to buy. But by taking even $50 out of each paycheque, you begin to build a small reserve of money for emergencies and big ticket items. If you start now and think of such savings as a bill to be paid, like your rent or cable or other regular monthly payment, you can start yourself on the road to good financial health. The easiest way to accomplish this pay-yourself-first technique is to arrange an automatic withdrawal from your chequing account into a savings account. Some people find is easier if they actually write a cheque for deposit to their savings account; others open this savings account at an out-of-the-way branch so there is less temptation to raid the account for everyday expenditures. Alternatively, you can set up a monthly savings plan with a mutual fund company. Funds are withdrawn from your bank account and used to purchase mutual fund units. You get the benefit of dollar cost averaging. You know yourself best – set up the savings plan in a way that suits your personal habits.

What about credit cards and loans?

It is important to start building a credit rating at this point, but often the temptation of a credit card is simply too much for the person just starting out. If you get into the habit of using a credit card now, you could be establishing some very bad habits, habits that are difficult to break. Of course, if you do need a credit card you must learn to use it wisely. Here are some tips to follow:

- Choose a credit card that can accomplish most of the transactions you will make on credit. Holding 10 or 15 different cards may look impressive, but it is much easier to lose track of what you have spent if there are many separate bills coming into the house.

- Stick to a pre-determined credit limit – pre-determined by you. A credit card company is not in the business of giving you credit for your convenience. They want you to owe money so they can charge you interest. There's a fine line between making your payments regularly and overspending. If you feel you can manage a $500 limit and only that, choose that limit. Often if you are punctual and pay off your bills regularly, a company will ask if they can raise your limit. It sounds like an honour to be offered a $5,000 limit, but it is in fact foolish unless your cash flow is such that you can and will pay off such an amount at the end of the month. That's the key – set your limit at what you can afford to pay off in full each month.

- Shop around for the best deal. Like most financial services now, there are a variety of credit cards to choose from, even among the same carriers. Decide what you need the card for, calculate your credit limit as well as the number of times you intend to use the card per month, and then compare the different packages available. Cost will be an important determinant.

- Pay off the outstanding balance every month. Better yet, set aside the money when it is charged. That way there will be no squirming at the end of the month to meet the payment.

You don't really like the idea of a young person having a credit card, I take it.

Credit is like gambling – it is addictive. It is easy to live the good life on credit, until it catches up with you. There are others ways of establishing a credit rating.

What about using credit to buy consumer products like a TV or computer? So many retailers have those special "Don't pay now! Pay later" come-ons. It's not like a credit card – it's like free credit.

It's not free credit. The cost of doing business is built into the price of the item you are purchasing. A retailer is in business to make money, so there are no free rides. It is not the retailer's fault or problem if a consumer overspends.

Let's say you want a new car and you arrange to buy it now and start paying for it in six months. Instead of buying a $10,000 car, you move up to a car worth $12,500 because you will save the first six months of car payments, and, of course, you will put that money aside in the interim. What really happens is that you spend the money on something else and still ending up owing the additional $2,500, so now you are out $5,000. This may not seem like a lot, but unless you are disciplined about your spending and saving habits, it is very easy to accumulate debt. So we are back to the $50 per paycheque savings scheme.

Phase Two – Marriage, Mortgage, Children

The late twenties to early forties phase is dominated by a series of first time happenings. It could include getting married (that settling down period your mother always talked about), buying a house and starting a family. While initially the investor is still adventurous, more responsibilities are being taken on. Work or job-related activities take on more importance, and leisure time activities tend to be replaced by house maintenance and family outings. Switching from freedom mode to family mode brings financial responsibilities and constraints.

Those who have started their $50 per paycheque plan may now have greater difficulty in saving, as there is always a new lawnmower, air conditioning or other household expense popping up. In fact, what little has been saved may already be spent. But maintaining this type of plan is more important than ever, if only for vacations and emergencies. Maintaining the discipline of saving regularly is vitally important as well.

Savings can be invested in various ways, although, for most, a high degree of liquidity is necessary to cover for emergencies and other contingencies. Speculative investments are usually not liquid, and any speculating should be viewed as an expense rather than an investment. You must accept upfront that there may be no return *on* your money and no return *of* the money invested. It has to be money that will cause little or no hardship if lost.

It is also time to start saving for your children's education. Whether or not one chooses a Registered Education Savings Plan, putting money away now when the children are young will certainly mean that paying for college or university later on does not break the bank.

If you haven't started saving money on a regular basis yet, it is not too late to start. These habits should be well-developed before moving into the next phases of the life cycle, when retirement and investment savings become more important than ever before.

Here again, using cash instead of credit whenever possible is important. While credit facilities like a credit card or overdraft protection at your banking institution are often necessary, you should avoid using this protection if you can.

Enzo, did you have a traumatic credit experience as a child? You seem so adamant that credit is bad!

Well, I did once lend fifty cents to my friend and he never paid me back. But credit in and of itself is not bad. The overuse of credit is bad, and it is very easy to get into the habit of using credit and becoming overextended. Still, how else could someone afford a house without a mortgage? At this stage in life it is important to have a good credit rating. But simply owing a lot of money for personal possessions such as a stereo or colour TV is not financially healthy. If you only use credit cards for short term needs and the money owing will be paid off promptly, it can make sense.

A friend of mine was in financial trouble a few years ago because of that very problem. She ended up declaring bankruptcy. It was really tough on her and her family. Getting a credit card now for her is a difficult proposition, but she doesn't really want one anymore. Talk about converted! She pays cash for everything! If she sees something she wants to buy, she waits two weeks before she buys it. That gives her a cooling off period before any new purchase. If in two weeks she still wants the item, if it is still there and she has the cash, she buys it. It's a time-consuming process but she's not stuck with a lot of worthless and unnecessary junk.

Phase Three – The Core Years: Moving Up Financially

The years from 40 to 55 are the most profitable for the income-earner, but could also be the most difficult. Mid-life crisis, possibly divorce and other personal problems are most likely to appear here. The mortgage may be paid off and the children finishing college, but there can be a possibility of job loss. This period of life often becomes a time for taking stock, as people look back over their lives to see what accomplishments and goals have been reached. For some, career changes or financial upheavals can occur. Stress can be a big problem. Added to all that is a sense of mortality.

With a lot of the financial responsibilities such as children's education expenses and a mortgage paid off, this may be the first opportunity that most people have to really save money for investment and retirement purposes. One of the biggest mistakes made at this point is taking too much risk in an effort to make up for lost opportunities. This is un-wise. Investments should be reasonably conservative, with speculation taking a back seat.   Money should increasingly be put aside for retirement purposes into Registered Retirement Savings Plans and company pension plans.

I'm self employed, so I don't have a company pension plan. I've started an RRSP, but I'd like to hear more about them.

RRSPs are perhaps the most important investment vehicle available to the average person. They were first developed in 1957, but it is only recently that RRSPs have become a battleground for every conceivable type of financial institution around.   Competition has heated up, as the marketing areas of these organizations realized what a gold mine this type of account can be to them. You should talk to your IA to find out what type of RRSP is best suited to you. As well, it has become somewhat of a truism that the Canada Pension Plan or its equivalent will be inadequate when the current generation of workers retires. This shouldn't come as a big surprise to any student of finance. People now collecting CPP did not fully fund their own pensions. Money for current expenditures is coming from current deposits. Will the govern-ment have enough income in the future to pay for CPP for the Baby Boom generation? I think of CPP really as a form of payroll tax. I am not counting on it to support me in my retirement.

So how do we plan for the future?

If you are working for a company that has one, a pension plan may provide well for your future. If you are a member of a pension plan you should carefully read the plan documents so you can understand exactly what you can expect to receive in the future. You should receive a document annually from the plan's administrators describing your expected income level at retirement, given your current level of contributions. You can then extrapolate the figures to come up with an income level upon your retirement. Watch for limits though. There may come a time when contributions do not add anything to your future pension income. Plans vary and since it is your money, you should pay close attention to any information you receive about your plan.

I've been told that a pension plan should take a back seat to RRSPs. There is the pension adjustment that reduces your RRSP contribution limit. You can get a bigger tax deduction if you just go the RRSP route.

Yes, if you belong to a pension plan, your RRSP limit is adjusted downward in an effort to equalize the non-pensionable employee and the pensionable employee. While it is possible to calculate your own pension adjustment, or PA, this information is sent to you by the government with your notice of assessment from last year's tax return. I would simply use their figures rather than bother to try to calculate the figure myself.

If you were to simply look at the RRSP contribution limit and compare it to the pension contribution, it would appear that the RRSP route is the best way to go. But often companies contribute to the pension plan on your behalf. If you were to go the RRSP route, you would lose this contribution. The second issue to consider is whether you are going to make use of the additional contribution limit allowed to the non-pensionable RRSP holder. If you cannot afford the additional RRSP contribution, it is a moot point whether one is better than the other. This decision is a personal one, and all permutations should be thought through. A pension plan is inaccessible – is this to your favour or is it a disadvantage? If you occasionally dip into the RRSP to pay bills, I would strongly recommend a pension over the RRSP. If you are disciplined, can afford the higher contributions, and can manage your RRSPs well, opt for the RRSP.

But regardless of whether you combine a pension with an RRSP for your retirement or only use an RRSP, start your contributions early. And if you can afford it, put in the total allowable contribution, and the one-time $2,000 allowable over-contribution. The overcontribution is not tax deductible – it is simply a deposit to your plan that is allowed to grow tax sheltered without penalty. RRSPs are tricky – there is a great deal of legislation surrounding the plan and its administration. Contributions have limits; overcontributions, over and above the lifetime $2,000 limit, are penalized. But if you put the $2,000 in now, it will grow tax sheltered and that is the main goal here.

You have used the terms tax deduction and tax sheltered. Can you clarify?

Your contribution or deposit to an RRSP is a tax deduction – it reduces your income level and therefore your taxes payable. Let's say your earned income is $40,000, so your RRSP contribution limit is 18% of this figure or $7,200. If you did contribute $7,200 to your RRSP, your taxable income would be reduced from $40,000 to $32,800. So the $7,200 is a tax deduction. As well, it is tax sheltered within the plan. That means that as this investment grows and earns income, no tax is payable. But tax is payable when you withdraw money from the plan, which you must do in the year you turn 69 if you haven't done it already. Withdrawals from an RRSP are taxed at your then current rates of income tax. You can roll over the contents of your RRSP into a Registered Retirement Income Fund or RRIF, which will further shelter your money.

RRSP Contribution Limits

18% of last year's earned income to a maximum of $13,500 in 1994, $14,500 in 1995 and $15,500 in 1996.

For example: if you earned $50,000 in 1993, your 1994 limit would be 18% or $9,000. But if your 1993 income was $85,000 your limit would be the 1994 maximum of $13,5000

Is there an upper limit to contribution levels for RRSPs?

There is a dollar limit as well as the 18% limit. The government has reduced the limit from the scheduled $15,500 to a maximum of $13,500 per year until 2004. You can carry unused contributions forward indefinately.

How should you invest your RRSP?

Some people believe that an RRSP should only include fixed income securities, so GICs and their ilk are acceptable investments. I disagree. If you have a large investment portfolio it makes sense to have your fixed income portion tax sheltered, as this type of investment is the most highly taxed. But if your investment portfolio is limited, some growth or equity exposure is appropriate here. If you just invest in fixed income you could become a victim of inflation.

Inflation means that a dollar invested today is worth less tomorrow, so an inflationary hedge like an equity investment becomes important.

That's right. Once you have an idea of what type of plan interests you, say, bond or equity based, you can choose between a managed plan like a mutual fund, or a self-directed plan. Either type can be purchased through your Investment Advisor. You can also buy an RRSP directly from a mutual fund company, although then you would be limited to that company's funds.

You can have as many RRSPs as you want. But remember that you want to simplify things for yourself. Ten or 15 different plans may become a bit of a headache and could be costly, too, if each plan charges a trustee or other fee.

I want to choose my own investments.

I thought you would prefer that method of investing, Jason. If you have confidence in your ability and you pay attention to the basics, this is a good method. But you and you alone will be responsible for your RRSP. The IA who holds the plan can help you, but you must make the final decisions yourself. Any penalties imposed on you by the government for violation of rules and regulations are your problem, not the investment dealer's. Make sure you get the information your need.

What about investing in the U.S. and abroad?

You can diversify your RRSP by holding up to 20% of it in foreign investments. The 20% limit is based on the book value of the investments; that is, what you paid for them. This usually requires a self-directed RRSP. Your IA should be able to help you determine your foreign content limits.

Of $1,000 contributed to an RRSP, $200 could be invested in foreign securities. If you've never held foreign securities in your RRSP, you could use 20% of the money previously invested (not 20% of the RRSP's current value) to buy them.

No wonder there are so many books on RRSP investing.

Yes, we've barely scratched the surface here. You should get more reading material from your financial institution or from the bookstore or library if you are going to maximize your RRSP and invest effectively.

I was thinking of using funds from my RRSP to buy a house. I might even use it to hold my mortgage. I've been putting money away for awhile – I would like access to it.

Borrowing from your RRSP for a downpayment is a government incentive program designed to attract people to the housing market. There are limits on who can participate and to what degree, and it does reduce your contribution limits.

If your RRSP holds the mortgage on your house, you must continue to make payments promptly or your RRSP can foreclose on you. You cannot give yourself a break on the mortgage rate either – it must be the market rate. There are administrative costs to pay as well. Generally, you can get a better return from another investment, and, after all, you want to generate the best returns possible for your retirement fund.

As well as making RRSP contributions, some initial estate planning should be started now to ensure that there are no surprises waiting in the wings. Problems can be worked out now, with the final details of an estate plan to be worked out later.

Phase Four – The Peak Years: Arriving

During the years from 55 to 65, investors can often add to their nest egg. More time is available to enjoy the hobbies developed after the kids left home. (Are they back yet?) Money should be coming in more quickly now as expenses continue to dwindle.

From an investment viewpoint, this should be a time to top-up any financial plans. RRSPs should be maximized, and other tax savings plans initiated so that every dollar counts. Investments should be increasingly conservative, with an eye to future retirement a few scant years away. If assets are large, plans for their distribution should be finalized. Again, people who at this point have still not instituted a regular savings plan may decide to invest what little they have accumulated in risky, go-for-broke ideas. This is foolhardy. Few investments can really make up for lost time and any investments should be well-considered. Losses should be taken very seriously, as there is no time to allow for recovery. If funds for retirement do not look adequate at this point, now is the time to make contingency plans. What can you do after retirement that can provide you with the funds you need? How can you arrange your affairs now to ensure that you can carry out those contingency plans?

Phase Five – The Calmer Years: Retirement and Beyond

If you have followed our plan, post-retirement years can be less stressful. However, as regular expenses drop, new ones may appear. Hobbies such as travelling, collecting and even gardening can all be additional costs not entirely anticipated by the retiree. But all in all, this should be a joyful time for sharing with one's family and friends.

Your investments should include enough liquidity to provide for cash needs. Investments should be conservative, but not exclusively in fixed income investments because of inflation. Inflation is the sworn enemy of anyone on a fixed income. Returns and inflation figures must be monitored regularly to minimize inflation's erosive affects. As well, the volatility of interest rates is such that diversification is particularly important.

Thank you for planning out the rest of my life, Enzo. Now I can relax.

Well, Jason, the life cycle approach can give you a framework of what your financial goals should be over time. It's not meant to be a definitive plan. This framework will be useful later when we talk about asset allocation.

One more aspect that should be discussed before we get into the planning process itself is risk. Risk is a popular topic in discussions about investments, but how can you gauge it? Try this – if you cannot sleep at night after purchasing an investment product, it is too risky for you. Just because your Aunt Hilda likes to dabble in penny mining stocks does not mean you should or indeed can, even if you can afford to lose your entire investment. Risk is a personal thing that you really must come to grips with yourself. Another way of gauging risk is by return. If an investment is touted as providing a 50% annualized return, guess what? There is risk, and a great deal of risk.

To get an idea of the risk/return trade-off, consider treasury bills. You recall that T-bills are money market instruments issued by the Government of Canada. They can mature at various times, up to one year. By virtue of the fact that they are issued by the government, with its powers of taxation, these investments are considered risk-free. So as a starting point for returns, looking at the current yield on a T-bill will tell you what a risk-free investment is paying. From here it is all relative. But realize that you will not get something for nothing. If someone offers you a return of 25% with no risk, you should run, not walk to the nearest exit. And if one GIC is paying a premium over another for the same period of time, ask yourself why. One company may need five-year money to match their loan portfolio and are paying a premium to attract it, but if the rates across all yield maturities are higher than those of other companies, the improvement in yield could really be a risk premium. Investing in such a GIC could be very risky; you could have another Principal Group in the making.

The Financial Planning Pyramid

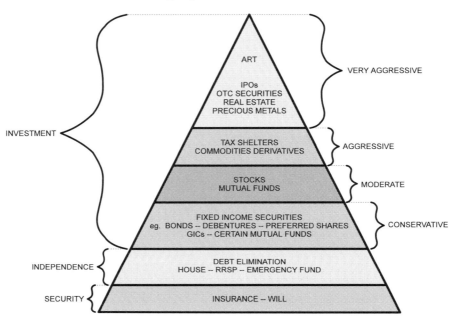

This illustration is meant as a guideline to the levels of risk you should be willing to accept in a specific type of investment. The base of your investment programme should be, in a manner of speaking, risk management. This should include a will, life insurance and property insurance.

Security

The first item in the financial pyramid is insurance – as gloomy, but as important as having a will.

Insurance

Insurance is a financial planning tool and should not be thought of as a way of replacing a loved one with money. Consider the following tale, a common one in the insurance sales pitch: the young couple with five children. The wife has given up a lucrative career to stay home with the children at least for the next 12 or 13 years. The husband, hardworking, loving and reliable, is tragically killed in a car accident, leaving an unemployed mate at home with the children, a mortgage and other bills to pay and no income and few assets. These kinds of stories tug at the heart strings, but we often dismiss such tragedy lightly. Well guess what? It could happen. Insurance is a difficult subject to talk about because it does put a price on our mortality.

There's good news and bad news about insurance. Death benefits, when payable to a named beneficiary and not an estate, are tax-free. Insurance creates an instant pool of money for the estate to pay off debts like a mortgage, car and personal loans, as well as to fund educational costs for children. The bad news is you won't be around to enjoy it yourself. So how much do you need?

To calculate this figure, simply remove from your budget your income and any expenses pertaining to you specifically. The amount of insurance required would equal your contribution to the household.

For example, your earnings may cover a mortgage and a personal loan totalling $125,000, while you also pay monthly expenses of $1,000. You may decide to buy enough insurance to cover the debt outstanding as well as enough to generate an income of $1,000 a month for the miscellaneous expenses. That could mean you will need approximately $250,000 in insurance.

Calculating the amount of insurance and deciding what type to buy go hand in hand. A reputable life insurance agent or broker can walk you through the steps necessary to come to a decision. Do not overlook benefits that may be available from work; you can often buy life insurance through your employer. But how secure is your job and, for that matter, your employer? This insurance may be convertible if and when you leave. Review this information before you buy additional coverage, and have the details available to the insurance sales person. Before you sign up for any insurance, read the information available on the policy to ensure that it is what you need, want, and can afford.

Disability insurance is a definite must for those unfortunate enough not to have this type of coverage through an employer. Insurance of this sort replaces income for a worker suffering from a long term illness or disability. It can be expensive for certain job categories. Again, a reputable insurance agent can explain the details of these types of plans. It is something worth discussing, especially with the growing trend in self-employment.

Other forms of insurance include home or apartment insurance. This is an often overlooked item with apartment dwellers. The need for such insurance usually hits home only after disaster – fire, theft or damage – has struck. Anyone who has experienced any one of these traumas knows the value of this risk management product. Protection is not overly expensive and the peace of mind it offers is well worth the price of admission.

Insurance: Term, Whole and Universal

There are two basic types of insurance — term insurance and whole life insurance.

Term insurance is temporary insurance that can provide protection for a limited time. It is inexpensive and is in essence a no-frills type of product. For some people, term is an adequate product that provides the coverage needed and no more. But term insurance does expire. The premiums for this type of insurance are not uniform — a 25-year old is going to pay a lot less than a 40-year old for the same amount of coverage. Because the need for insurance varies during your life, some people feel that term insurance is an appropriate choice — you can purchase large amounts when family responsibilities make the need for protection greatest, and then purchase smaller amounts with the same dollar premium at a later stage. For the disciplined financial planner, term does make sense, but for those who have difficulty saving, whole life insurance is a possibility.

Whole life is permanent insurance. It does not expire but rather will provide death benefits unless cancelled. The premium on the whole life insurance policy remains the same throughout its lifespan. The policy accumulates a cash surrender value, usually after five years, and can become an asset. A whole life policy can be borrowed against or used as collateral for a loan, so can be considered an investment. However, it doesn't stand up well on its investment merits alone — returns are generally poor.

Because term can replace whole life insurance, it is often suggested that it is better that whole life. Some financial pundits advise the investor to purchase term and put the difference between the price of term and whole life into a savings account. This is a good idea if it is done consistently.

Insurance companies have come up with a product that replicates this type of investment/insurance product. It is called universal life. This is a very flexible policy which really is a combination savings plan and life insurance policy. You pay a premium for the insurance and also deposit a sum of money into a savings account. The deposit and the premiums can be very flexible, to suit an individual budget. They can be changed if necessary, as long as there is enough cash in the savings portion of the policy to pay for the life insurance premium. This is a great type of policy for certain individuals, and can be an effective estate planning tool.

I agree. Several years ago, my apartment was severely damaged in a fire. And, you know, one of the most expensive things to replace was my wardrobe. Furniture and other possessions were easily replaceable, but my clothing! I just never knew how expensive it could be to replace all my winter and summer clothing, boots, shoes – everything!

Sounds like you had a good insurance policy with a replacement value clause. This clause ensures that you can replace your personal items at today's cost, not the cost which you originally paid. It may not be important for something like an electronic item where price levels have declined, but for clothes and other personal possessions, such a clause is worth the expense.

Wills

A will is simply a necessity. While most people have a great deal of difficulty in dealing with the inevitability of their own death, immortality is not granted to those without wills. Leaving your family at the mercy of the court system is reckless. While each province has its own laws governing the situation of dying intestate – without a will – rest assured that there is no guarantee that your wishes or anything like your wishes will be carried out upon your death if you do not have a will telling people how you want your assets disposed of. When you die without a will, the state steps in and decides what is best for your family. A portion of your assets would go to your spouse, with the balance passed on to your children, to be administered by the Official Guardian as appointed by the courts. If your spouse requires additional monies for the children from the estate, they must petition the courts to prove need. As well, investment decisions would be made by the Official Guardian. And this in itself should scare you into preparing a will, for we all know how well governments have managed their financial affairs in the last two or three decades. If you have no spouse or child, all assets would be transferred to surviving parents. Save your family or survivors a great deal of grief and prepare a will.

Wills

A will is a legal document that instructs your survivors how your affairs are to be settled after your death. It must contain certain information about you and it must name an executor, the person whom you charge with settling your affairs on your behalf. A will should be drawn up with the aid of a lawyer. Although a holograph will (one that is written in your own handwriting) can be valid as well, it is not recommended. One copy of the will usually remains in the possession of the lawyer; another copy kept with your financial information papers. The following is a partial list of the items that could be included in a will. If you are using a lawyer, prepare this information prior to your first meeting to ensure that none of your wishes are mistaken or left out altogether.

1) The Testator or person making the will must be clearly identified by name and complete address. All previous wills must be revoked.

2) The executor must be named. (Be sure to inform the person you have chosen. Better yet, discuss their willingness to take on this responsibility prior to springing it on them.)

3) Name a guardian for your children.

4) State any specific bequests or gifts, personal property or money.

5) Give instructions as to what to do with the remainder of the estate, e.g. does it pass on to your spouse or children?

Some people also include instructions on the care of their children and how their guardian is to spend any monies for their education and upkeep. If the executor and guardians are well-chosen, there should be less need for detailed instructions. Flexibility for both of these parties is often more desirable that a rigid, difficult-to-administer estate that puts no faith in these people.

Independence

The next level of the pyramid involves buying a house and setting up your long-range retirement plans, as well as an emergency fund.

An emergency fund is a pool of liquid assets in a savings account or near-cash equivalents. The fund should equal about three to six months of living expenses, including mortgage payments, groceries, utilities, and other payables. This fund is for those worst-case scenarios: what if you became seriously ill for an extended period of time? Do you have disability insurance that would cover your drop in income and when does it kick in? If there is a problem in receiving benefits due you, can you and your family survive until the money comes in? Being seriously ill brings with it enough hardship and suffering without having to wonder when your benefit plan will kick in. The emergency fund can see you through such dark periods.

Another more commonplace happening in today's job market is a layoff or plant closure. While we have excellent social safety nets in Canada, it is wise to have some money put aside for a rainy day.

It is best to eliminate any debts before advancing to the next steps in the pyramid. Some debt may be accrued when purchasing an RRSP. Borrowing to invest in one is not such a bad idea if you can afford the cost of the loan. Better yet, you should perhaps think of making double "payments", using one to pay off the loan for the current RRSP contribution and saving the other as next year's contribution.

For most people, owning a house is a major goal and can become the cornerstone of their financial plan. It is the most significant asset they own. The best advice for anyone purchasing a house is to go slow. Don't be talked into assuming too large a mortgage that you "can grow into". If you overbuy, you run the risk of losing any equity you may put into the house. It is better to underbuy so that you can afford to save money for your retirement, travel or any other enjoyable hobby. A modest yet affordable home is certainly more enjoyable that a house just a bit too expensive that causes grief every month at mortgage payment time.

Investments

The other section of the pyramid represents accepted wisdom on the levels of risk in other types of investment products. This is merely a representation though, and each investment should be reviewed on its own merits. For example, a deep discount or junk bond, because it is a bond, would be considered by this table as a conservative investment. But this is simply not the case. These bonds are extremely volatile and are more like an option purchase than a GIC or other fixed income investment.

Let's review what we've accomplished so far. You have done your best to cover all the necessities of life to secure your family's welfare. This is the security base of the pyramid.

Second, you have built up cash reserves. Such reserves can include the house, RRSP, and an emergency cash fund for liquidity.

Last but not least is the growth part of your investment plan. If all goes well, here is where you can accumulate savings to fund the better things in life!

But it appears to me that the life cycle and the pyramid are incongruous. A 20- year old can purchase risky assets under the life cycle plan, but if you following the pyramid, you would probably put that risk money into an emergency fund.

That's true. It is reasonable for a younger person just starting out to put money into risky assets. Remember that these are guidelines only. Sometimes the lure of a once-in-a-lifetime investment is too tempting to ignore. The pyramid is one approach to investing. It is a good one, as it is conservative and serves as a logical progression thought the available investment products. On the other hand, the life cycle approach is more like a series of signposts. How you fit these two pieces of the financial planning puzzle together is your personal financial plan.

The last bit of planning you have to do is to set down a list of goals or objectives. These could be anything from arranging to pay off outstanding credit card bills to saving for a house. It is not wrong to have these as simultaneous goals, depending on the interest rate on the credit outstanding. Writing these goals down though, lends a degree of urgency and importance to them. It also lets you evaluate later how close you have come to meeting them. You should have short, mid and long-term financial goals listed. Keep all your paperwork together; your written goals should be kept with your other financial information lists.

Plan on at least one review a year. Update all your records as well as your list of goals. Monitor your progress and make any necessary adjustments. Do not leave plans in place that are at odds with your goals. It is probably a good idea to review your will and your insurance policy to ensure that these two items are still adequate and continue to reflect your wishes. It is amazing how easy it is to neglect such documents in the face of very changed circumstances.

What Can Go Wrong

There are many things that can disrupt a financial plan, natural disasters not included. These four are perhaps the most damaging.

- Inflation ⇨ as we found out a few weeks ago, inflation is the enemy of bonds. Inflation implies a general rise in consumer prices and means that a dollar is just not a dollar any more. Creeping inflation is perhaps the most dangerous form of this rather insidious financial disease. Small and constant price increases are easily adjusted to and by the time you realize the effect on a particular fixed income investment, it can be too late to react. On the other hand, such inflation can lead to buoyant stock markets. Borrowers fare well in inflationary times as they pay back their debt with cheaper dollars. Lenders can suffer greatly.

- Unemployment ⇨ losing your job can be devastating. Emergency funds can help to alleviate financial problems.

- Disability ⇨ the proper insurance policy, company benefit or privately purchased, can take care of the financial aspect of this problem.

One last point that can cause any well prepared financial plan to fail – lack of follow-through. It does not matter how much planning you do if it is not actively followed and supported. As we mentioned at the start, make sure your final plan is:

- do-able;

- flexible;

- not intimidating;

- able to allow for some rewards, too.

If your plan can meet these criteria you should easily be on the way to financial success.

What's next?

The next step is up to you. These seminars have tried to give you a good foundation on which to build your investing activities. You may not feel ready to strike out entirely on your own, but you should be able to properly evaluate the information and advice that your IA gives you. Whether you choose to operate on your own or work closely with your IA, the knowledge you have acquired here will lead to better investment decisions and better results over the long term.

The bibliography appears after the glossary.

But this is just the beginning. There is always more to learn, and to that end we are providing you with a bibliography. You also have to keep an eye on the rapid changes that are part of the securities markets – the bibiography includes a review of current sources of information. Finally, you can always take another course!

Summary

Although the range of investment possibilities is the same for everybody, your personal circumstances determine what will be attractive to you. This is why financial plans will vary from person to person.

In developing a financial plan, you must first establish your current financial position. This means preparing a balance sheet and income statement for yourself. You can then use the life cycle approach to help you develop a suitable range of investments. There are some situations that are common to us all at certain stages of life, and the life cycle approach can be useful in putting together an appropriate investment strategy. Opening an RRSP is a suitable strategy at any stage, with the preferred time being earlier rather than later.

The financial planning pyramid can also be used to determine priorities. Insurance and will preparation form the base of the pyramid and should be attended to before moving up to the other levels. Buying a house, setting up an RRSP, putting aside emergency funds and reducing or eliminating debt form the next stage. Additional funds can then be used to generate investment growth.

Because a financial plan depends on personal circumstances and because these can change, the plan must be reviewed on a regular basis. At the same time, review your will and insurance policy. These documents will only work in your favour if they reflect your current circumstances and wishes.

Financial Information

List of Financial Institutions / *Advisors*

Name of Institution	**Account Number**	**Contact:** Name & Phone

Chequing Account
1. _____   _____   _____
2. _____   _____   _____

Savings Account
1. _____   _____   _____
2. _____   _____   _____

RRSP Account
1. _____   _____   _____
2. _____   _____   _____
3. _____   _____   _____

Insurance (Personal)
1. _____   _____   _____
2. _____   _____   _____

Property and Car Insurance
1. _____   _____   _____
2. _____   _____   _____

Investment Advisors
1. _____   _____   _____
2. _____   _____   _____

Mutual Funds
1. _____   _____   _____
2. _____   _____   _____
3. _____   _____   _____

Credit Cards   **Issuer**
1. _____   _____   _____
2. _____   _____   _____
3. _____   _____   _____

Lawyer _____   Phone: _____

Accountant _____   Phone: _____

Other _____   Phone: _____

Social Insurance Number: _____

Net Worth

Date _____

ASSETS
Current Assets

Cash & Cash Equivalents
Chequing Account(s) _____
Savings Account(s) _____
CSBs _____

Short-term Investments (current value)
T-bills _____
Money Market Funds _____
Other Similar Deposits _____

Cash Surrender Value of Life Insurance _____

Total Current Assets _____

Longer-term Investments (current value)
Interest Bearing Certificates _____
Stocks _____
Mutual Funds _____
Tax Shelters _____
Other Investments _____
RRSPs _____
Pension Plans _____
Other _____

Other Assets
House _____
Car _____
Art _____
Personal Belongings (jewellery) _____
Other

Total Assets _____

LIABILITIES

Short-term Debt

Credit Cards _____

Personal Loans _____

Other Short-term Liabilities _____

Total Short-term Liabilities _____

Longer-term Liabilities

Mortgage _____

Other Long-term Liabilities _____

Total Long-term Liabilities _____

Total Liabilities _____

NET WORTH (Assets - Liabilities) _____

Income Statement

INCOME

Employment Income

_____   _____

_____   _____

Commissions / Bonus

_____   _____

_____   _____

Other (self-employed)

_____   _____

_____   _____

Total   _____

Investment Income

Interest   _____

Dividends   _____

Rental Income   _____

Other _____   _____

_____   _____

Total   _____

Income from all Sources   _____

EXPENSES

Housing

Mortgage (Rent)   _____

Taxes   _____

Insurance   _____

Maintenance   _____

Utilities   _____

Other Costs   _____

Total   _____

Personal Expenses
　　Food　　　　　　　　　　_____
　　Clothing　　　　　　　　_____
　　Life Insurance　　　　　_____
　　Hobby Expenses　　　　_____
　　Other　　　　　　　　　_____

Total　　　　　　　　　　　　　_____

Transportation
　　Car　　　　　　　　　　　_____
　　Gas　　　　　　　　　　　_____
　　Maintenance　　　　　　_____

Total　　　　　　　　　　　　　_____

Other
　　Savings　　　　　　　　　_____
　　Charity　　　　　　　　　_____
　　RRSP　　　　　　　　　　_____

Total　　　　　　　　　　　　　_____

Other Expenses　　　　　　　_____

Total Expenses　　　　　　　　　_____

TOTAL INCOME LESS TOTAL EXPENSES*

*This amount should be set aside for future expenditures.

Glossary

Note: words in **bold face** (dark) type within definitions have their own glossary definition.

Acceptance Paper: A colloquial term for short-term promissory notes issued by sales finance companies to fund loans to consumers for cars, appliances, etc. (See **Finance Company Paper**.)

Accounts payable: Debts owed by a company for goods or services purchased that are payable within one year. A **current liability** on the **Balance Sheet**.

Accounts receivable: Debts owed to a company for goods or services it has sold for which payment is expected within one year. A **current asset** on the **Balance Sheet**.

Accrued Interest: Interest accumulated on a bond or debenture since the last interest payment date.

Acquisition Fee: See **Load**.

Affiliated Company: A company with less than 50% of its shares owned by another corporation, or one whose stock, with that of another corporation, is owned by the same controlling interests.

American Depository Receipts (ADRs): A system devised by the American investment community whereby the original stock **certifi-**

cate of a foreign security is registered in the name of an American trust company or a U.S. bank and held in safekeeping by them. The trust company or bank then issues receipts against this stock, and these are traded as ADRs. The system developed because purchasers of foreign securities found that it could take several months to have foreign stock issues registered in their name.

Amortization: Gradually writing off the value of an intangible asset over a period of time. Commonly applied to items such as goodwill, improvements to leased premises, or expenses of a new stock or bond issue.

Annual Report: The formal financial statements and report on operations issued by a company to its shareholders after its fiscal year-end.

Arbitrage: The simultaneous purchase of a security on one stock exchange and the sale of the same security on another exchange at prices which yield a profit to the arbitrageur.

Arrears: Interest or dividends which were not paid when due but are still owed.

Assets: Everything a company or a person owns or has owed to it. A **Balance Sheet** category.

Associated Company: A company owned jointly by two or more other companies.

Averages and Indices: Statistical tools that measure the state of the stock market or the economy, based on the performance of stocks or other meaningful components, e.g. the Dow Jones Industrial Average, the TSE 300 Composite Index, The Montreal Exchange Portfolio Index and the Consumer Price Index.

Averaging: See **Dollar Cost Averaging**.

Averaging Down: Buying more of a security at a lower price than the original investment. Aim: to reduce the average cost per unit. (See **Dollar Cost Averaging**.)

Balance Sheet: A financial statement showing a company's assets, liabilities and shareholders' equity on a given date.

Balloon: In some **serial bond** issues an extra-large amount may mature in the final year of the series – the "balloon".

Bank Rate: The minimum rate at which the Bank of Canada makes short-term advances to the chartered banks, other members of the **Canadian Payments Association** and investment dealers who are money market "jobbers". Since 1980 the Bank Rate has been set at ¼ of 1% (25 **basis points**) above the weekly average tender rate of 91-day Government of Canada treasury bills.

Bankers' Acceptance: A type of short-term negotiable commercial paper issued by a non-financial corporation but guaranteed as to principal and interest by its bank. The guarantee results in a higher issue price and consequent lower yield.

Banking Group: A group of investment firms, each of which individually assumes financial responsibility for part of an underwriting. (See **Underwriting**.)

Bankrupt: The legal status of an individual or company which is unable to pay its creditors and whose assets are therefore administered for its creditors by a Trustee in Bankruptcy.

Basis Point: A phrase used to describe differences in bond yields, with one basis point representing one-hundredth of a percentage point. Thus, if Bond X yields 11.50% and Bond Y 11.75%, the difference is 25 basis points.

Bear: One who expects that the market generally or the market price of a particular security will decline. (See also **Bull**.)

Bear Market: A declining market.

Bearer Security: A security (stock or bond) which does not have the owner's name recorded in the books of the issuing company nor on the security itself and which is payable to the holder, i.e. the possessor. (See also **Registered Security**.)

Beneficial Owner: The real owner of shares (or other assets). An investor may own shares which are registered in the name of a broker, trustee or bank to facilitate transfer or to preserve anonymity, but the investor would be the *beneficial* owner.

***Best Efforts* Underwriting**: The underwriter agrees to use his best efforts to sell a new issue of securities, but does not guarantee to the issuing company that any or all of the issue will be sold. The underwriter acts as an agent for the issuer in distributing the issue to his clients.

Between-Dealer Market: See **Over-the-Counter**.

Bid and Asked Quotations: Bid represents the highest price a prospective buyer is willing to pay; asked price is the lowest price the seller will accept. The two together are referred to as a *quotation* or *quote*.

Blue Chip: An active, leading, nationally known common stock with a record of continuous dividend payments and other strong investment qualities.

Blue Sky: A slang term for laws that various Canadian provinces and American states have enacted to protect the public against securities frauds. The term *blue skied* is used to indicate that a new issue has been cleared by a Securities Commission and may be distributed.

Board Lot: A regular trading unit which has uniformly been decided upon by stock exchanges. (See also **Odd Lot**.)

Bond: A **certificate** evidencing a debt on which the issuer promises to pay the holder a specified amount of interest for a specified length of time, and to repay the loan on its maturity. Strictly speaking, assets are pledged as security for a bond issue, except in the case of government "bonds", but the term is often loosely used to describe any funded debt issue.

Book Value: The amount of net assets belonging to the owners of a business (or shareholders of a company) based on balance sheet values.

Bought Deal: A new issue of stocks or bonds bought from the issuer by an investment dealer, frequently acting alone, for resale to its clients, usually by way of a private placement or short form prospectus. The dealer risks his own capital in the bought deal. In the event that the price has to be lowered to sell out the issue, the dealer absorbs the loss.

Broadened Base Earnings: A concept whereby the earnings per share of a company are computed to include a pro rata share of the earnings of all unconsolidated subsidiaries and associated companies.

Bull: One who expects that the market generally or the market price of a particular security will rise. (See also **Bear**.)

Bull Market: A rising market.

Business Days: See **Day**: **Business Day**.

Buy-ins: If a client or a dealer fails to deliver securities sold to another dealer within a specified number of days after the value (settlement) date, the receiving dealer may *buy-in* the securities in the open market and charge the client or the delivering dealer the cost of such purchases. (See also **Fails**.)

Call: See **Option** and **Puts and Calls**.

Callable: May be redeemed (called in) upon due notice by the security's issuer.

Call Loan: A loan which may be terminated or *called* at any time by the lender or borrower. Used to finance purchases of securities.

Canadian Investor Protection Fund: A fund set up by the stock exchanges and the Investment Dealers Association to protect investors from losses resulting from the bankruptcy of a Member firm.

Canadian Payments Association: Established in the 1980 revision of the Bank Act, this association operates a highly automated national clearing system for interbank payments. Members include chartered banks, trust and loan companies and some credit unions and caisses.

Capital: Has two distinct but related meanings. To an economist, it means machinery, factories and inventory required to produce other products. To an investor, it may mean the total of the financial assets that have been invested in securities, a home and other fixed assets, plus cash.

Capital Cost Allowance: An amount allowed under the Income Tax Act to be deducted from the value of certain assets and treated as an expense in computing an individual's or company's income for a taxation year. It may differ from the amount charged for the period in depreciation accounting.

Capital Gain or Loss: The profit or loss resulting from the sale of a capital asset. Tax consequences may result.

Capital Stock: All shares representing ownership of a company, including preferred as well as common.

Capitalization or Capital Structure: Total dollar amount of all debt, preferred and common stock, contributed surplus and retained earnings of a company. Can also be expressed in percentage terms.

Capitalize: Recording an expenditure initially as an asset on the **Balance Sheet** rather than as an **Earnings Statement** expense, and then writing it off or amortizing it (as an **Earnings Statement** expense) over a period of years. Examples include capitalized leases, interest, and research and development.

Cash Flow: A company's net income for a stated period plus any deductions that are not paid out in actual cash, such as **depreciation** and **amortization**, **deferred income taxes**, and **minority interest**.

Central Bank: A body established by a national Government to regulate currency and monetary policy on a national-international level. In Canada, it is the Bank of Canada; in the United States, the Federal Reserve Board; in the U.K., the Bank of England.

Certificate: The document evidencing ownership of a bond, stock or other security.

Certificate of Deposit (CD): A fixed-income debt security issued by most chartered banks, usually in minimum denominations of $ 1,000 with maturity terms of one to six years.

Charting: See **Technical Analysis**.

Class A and B Stock: Class A stock is often similar to a participating preferred share with a prior claim over Class B for a stated amount of dividends or assets or both, but without voting rights; the Class B usually has voting rights but no priority as to dividends or assets. Note that these distinctions do not always apply.

Clear Day: See **Day: Business Day**.

Closed-end Investment Company: See **Investment Company**.

Collateral: Securities or other property pledged by a borrower as a guarantee for repayment of a loan.

Collateral Trust Bond: A bond secured by stocks or bonds of companies controlled by the issuing company, or other securities, which are deposited with a trustee.

Comfort Letter: A letter filed with applicable Securities Commission(s) by a company's auditor when submitting unsigned financial statements for use in a **prospectus**. The letter says that the final format of the statements should not be materially different from those presently being filed. A letter is needed because the auditor does not sign his report before or when the financial statements are filed with the preliminary prospectus. The signing is done after the Securities Commission(s) has reviewed the prospectus and any required changes have been made.

Commercial Paper: Short-term negotiable debt securities issued by non-financial corporations with terms of a few days to a year.

Commission: The fee charged by a stock broker for buying or selling securities as agent on behalf of a client.

Common Stock: Securities representing ownership in a company and carrying voting privileges.

Company: See **Corporation**.

Compound Interest: Interest earned on an investment at periodic intervals and added to the amount of the investment; future interest payments are then calculated and paid at the original rate but on the increased total of the investment. In simple terms, interest paid on interest.

Confirmation: A printed acknowledgement giving details of a purchase or sale of a security which is normally mailed to a client by the broker or investment dealer within 24 hours of an order being executed. Also called a *contract*.

Conglomerate: A company directly or indirectly operating in a variety of industries, usually unrelated to each other. Conglomerates often acquire outside companies through the exchange of their own shares for the shares of the majority owners of the outside companies.

Consolidated Financial Statements: A combination of the financial statements of a parent company and its subsidiaries, presenting the financial position of the group as a whole.

Consolidation: See **Reverse Split**.

Constrained Share Companies: Include Canadian banks, trust, insurance, broadcasting and communication companies having constraints on the transfer of shares to persons who are not Canadian citizens or not Canadian residents.

Continuous Disclosure: In Ontario, a **reporting issuer** must issue a press release as soon as a **material change** occurs in its affairs and, in any event, within ten days. (See also **Timely Disclosure**.)

Contra Order: See **Cross on the Board**.

Contract: See **Confirmation**.

Contributed Surplus: A component of Shareholders' **Equity** which originates from sources other than earnings, such as the initial sale of stock above **par value**.

Convertible: A bond, debenture or preferred share which may be exchanged by the owner, usually for the common stock of the same company, in accordance with the terms of the conversion privilege. A company can force conversion by calling in such shares for **redemption** if the redemption price is below the market price.

Corporation or Company: A form of business organization created under provincial or federal statutes which has a legal identity separate from its owners. The corporation's owners (shareholders) have no liability for its debts. (See also **Limited Liability**.)

Country Banks: A colloquial term for non-bank lenders who provide short-term sources of credit for investment dealers; e.g. corporations, insurance companies and other institutional short-term investors, none of whom is under the jurisdiction of The Bank Act. (See also **Purchase and Resale Agreement**.)

Coupon: A portion of a **bond certificate** entitling the holder to an interest payment of a specified amount when clipped and presented at a bank on or after its due date.

Cover: Buying a security previously sold short. (See also **Short Sale**.)

Cross on the Board: Also called a **put-through** or **contra** order. When a broker has both an order to sell and an order to buy the same stock at the same price, a *cross* is allowed on the exchange floor without interfering with the limits of the prevailing market.

Cum Dividend: With **dividend**. If you buy shares quoted cum dividend, i.e. before the ex dividend date, you will receive an upcoming already-declared dividend. If shares are quoted **ex dividend** (without dividend) you are not entitled to the declared dividend.

Cum Rights: With **rights**. Buyers of shares quoted cum rights, i.e. before the ex rights date, are entitled to forthcoming already-declared rights. If shares are quoted **ex rights** (without rights) the buyer is not entitled to receive the declared rights.

Cumulative Preferred: A preferred stock having a provision that if one or more of its **dividends** are not paid, the unpaid dividends accumulate and must be paid before any dividends may be paid on the company's common shares.

Current Assets: Cash and assets which in the normal course of business would be converted into cash, usually within a year, e.g. **accounts receivable**, inventories. A **Balance Sheet** category.

Current Liabilities: Money owed and due to be paid within a year, e.g. **accounts payable.** A **Balance Sheet** category.

Current Return: The annual income from an investment expressed as a percentage of the investment's current value. On stock, calculated by dividing yearly dividend by market price; on bonds, by dividing yearly interest by current price.

Current Yield: See **Current Return**.

CUSIP: (Committee on Uniform Security Identification Procedures) is the trademark for a standard system of securities identification (i.e. CUSIP numbering system) and securities description (i.e. CUSIP descriptive system) that is used in processing and recording securities transactions in North America.

Cyclical Stock: One in an industry that is particularly sensitive to swings in economic conditions.

Day: **Business Day** – Refers to those days when most corporate and government offices are open for business, generally excluding weekends and holidays. **Calendar Day** – Refers to any day of the year. **Clear Day** – Under Ontario take-over legislation, if a stated period of days ends on a Sunday or a holiday, the period is extended to the next day that is not a Sunday or holiday.

Day Order: An order to buy or sell a security valid only for the day the order is given.

Debenture: A **certificate** of indebtedness of a government or company backed only by the general credit of the issuer and unsecured by mortgage or lien on any specific asset.

Debt: Money borrowed from lenders for a variety of corporate purposes. The borrower pays interest for the use of the money and is obligated to repay it at a set date.

Deemed Disposition: Under certain circumstances, taxation rules state that a transfer of property has occurred, even without a purchase or sale, e.g. there is a deemed disposition on death or emigration from Canada.

Default: A bond is in default when the borrower has failed to live up to its obligations under the trust deed with regard to interest and sinking fund payments or has failed to redeem the bonds at maturity.

Defensive Stock: A stock of a company with a record of stable earnings and continuous dividend payments and which has demonstrated relative stability in poor economic conditions.

Deferred Income Taxes: Income tax that would otherwise be payable currently, but which is deferred by using larger allowable deductions in calculating taxable income than those used in calculating net income in the financial statements. An acceptable practice, it is usually the result of timing differences and represents differences in accounting reporting guidelines and tax reporting guidelines.

Deficiency Letter: A Securities Commission letter sent to a company submitting a preliminary **prospectus** on a contemplated new issue of the company's securities. The letter poses any questions the Commission wants answered, and outlines any recommendations for changes. When all points raised in the letter are resolved, the issue's final prospectus is filed.

Delist: Removal of a security's listing on a stock exchange.

Delivery: **Delayed Delivery** – A transaction in which there is a clear understanding that delivery of the securities involved will be delayed beyond the normal settlement period. **Good Delivery** – When a security that has been sold is in proper form to transfer title by delivery to the buyer. **Regular Delivery** – Unless otherwise stipulated, sellers of stock must deliver it on or before the fifth business day after the sale. (See **Day**.)

Depletion: Refers to consumption of natural resources which are part of a company's assets. Producing oil, mining and gas companies deal in products that cannot be replenished and as such are known as *wasting assets*. The recording of depletion is a bookkeeping entry similar to **depreciation** and does not involve the expenditure of cash.

Depreciation: Systematic charges against earnings to write off the cost of an asset over its estimated useful life because of wear and tear through use, action of the elements, or obsolescence. It is a bookkeeping entry and does not involve the expenditure of cash.

Dilution: Reducing the actual or potential earnings per share by issuing more shares or giving options to obtain them.

Direct and Indirect Holdings: The holding(s) of an individual or company in other companies. For example: Company A owns 500,000 of Company B's 1,000,000 outstanding shares. Company A therefore has a 50% *direct* interest in Company B. Company B, in turn, owns 300,000 of Company C's outstanding 500,000 shares. Company B therefore has a 60% *direct* interest in Company C. Company A (by virtue of its 50% *direct* interest in Company B) has a 30% *indirect* interest in Company C.

Director: Person elected by voting common shareholders at the annual meeting to direct company policies.

Disaster Out Clause: A clause in an **underwriting** agreement allowing the underwriter to rescind the agreement, should a law, event or major financial occurrence transpire that adversely affects financial markets in general or the issuer in particular.

Disclaimer Clause: Securities Commissions require that all **prospectuses** carry on their front page the disclaimer that the Commission itself has in no way approved the merits of the securities being offered for sale.

Discount: The amount by which a preferred stock or bond sells below its **par value**.

Discounted: When some anticipated event such as increased dividends or lower earnings has already been reflected in the market price of a stock, it is said to be "already discounted" by the market.

Discretionary Account: A securities account where the client has given specific written authorization to a partner, director or qualified portfolio manager to select securities and execute trades for him. (See also **Managed Account** and **Wrap Account**.)

Diversification: Spreading investment risk by buying different securities in different companies in different kinds of businesses and/or locations.

Dividend: An amount distributed out of a company's profits to its shareholders in proportion to the number of shares they hold. Over the years a **preferred dividend** will remain at a fixed annual amount. The amount of **common dividends** may fluctuate with the company's profits. A company is under no legal obligation to pay preferred or common dividends.

Dollar Cost Averaging: Investing a fixed amount of dollars in a specific security at regular set intervals over a period of time, thereby reducing the average cost paid per unit. (See also **Averaging Down**.)

Dow Theory: A theory of market analysis based upon the performance of the Dow Jones Industrial and Transportation Averages. The theory is that the market is in a basic upward trend if one of these averages advances above a previous important high, accompanied or followed by a similar advance in the other. When both averages dip below previous important lows, this is regarded as confirmation of a basic downward trend.

Draft Prospectus: A prospectus prepared for internal use and discussion by the company issuing securities and the underwriters. It is not for outside distribution and shows only basic data on the company with little final detail about the terms of the planned **underwriting**. It is not a legal document and does not have to be drawn up strictly to Securities Commission standards. It is an earlier version of a preliminary prospectus and cannot be used in offering the security.

Earnings or Income Statement: A financial statement which shows a company's revenues and expenditures resulting in either a profit or a loss during a financial period.

Earnings Per Share: The portion of net income for a period attributable to a single common share of a company.

Equity or Shareholders' Equity: Ownership interest of common and preferred stockholders in a company. The difference between the **assets** and **liabilities** of a company which is sometimes called *net worth*. Equity divided by number of shares outstanding gives equity per share.

Equity Earnings: A company's share of an unconsolidated subsidiary's earnings. The equity accounting method is used when a company owns 20% to 50% of a subsidiary.

Escrowed or Pooled Shares: Outstanding shares of a company which, while entitled to vote and receive dividends, may not be bought or sold unless special approval is obtained. This technique is commonly used by mining and oil companies when **treasury shares** are issued for new properties. Shares can be released from escrow (i.e. freed to be bought and sold) only with the permission of applicable authorities such as a stock exchange and/or securities commission.

Ex Dividend or Rights: Without dividend or rights. The opposite of cum. (See **Cum Dividend** and **Cum Rights**.)

Exchange Fund Account: A special federal government account operated by the Bank of Canada to hold and conduct transactions in Canada's foreign exchange reserves on instructions from the Minister of Finance.

Exempt List: Large professional buyers of securities, mostly financial institutions, that are offered a portion of a new issue by one member of the **banking group** on behalf of the whole syndicate.

Exempt Market: An unregulated market for sophisticated participants in government bonds, corporate issues and commercial paper. A **prospectus** has not been required to raise money privately from private investors (largely institutions, but also individuals) and registration with a securities commission for those so dealing has not been needed.

Exempt Purchaser: A category of institutional investors to which the sale of a new issue of securities does not require the issuer to file a **prospectus** with the applicable securities commission.

Extendible Bond or Debenture: A bond or debenture with terms granting the holder the option to extend the maturity date by a specified number of years.

Extra: The short form of *extra dividend*. A dividend in the form of stock or cash in addition to the regular common dividend the company has been paying.

Face Value: The value of a bond or debenture that appears on the face of the **certificate**. Face value is ordinarily the amount the issuer will pay at maturity. Face value is no indication of market value.

Fails: Short for failed deliveries. Failure to deliver a security on **Settlement Date**.

Final Prospectus: The prospectus which supersedes the preliminary prospectus and is accepted for filing by applicable provincial securities commissions. The final prospectus shows all required information pertinent to the new issue and a copy must be given to each first-time buyer of the new issue.

Finance or Acceptance Company Paper: Short-term negotiable debt securities similar to **Commercial Paper**, but issued by finance companies.

Financial Intermediary: An institution such as a bank, life insurance company, credit union or mutual fund which receives cash, which it invests, from suppliers of capital.

Firm Bid - Firm Offer: An undertaking to buy (firm bid) or sell (firm offer) a specified amount of securities at a specified price for a specified period of time, unless released from this obligation by the seller in the case of a firm bid or the buyer in the case of a firm offer.

Fiscal Agent: An investment dealer appointed by a company or government to advise it in financial matters and to manage the underwriting of its securities.

Fiscal Policy: The policy pursued by the federal government to direct the economy through taxation and the level and allocation of government spending.

Fiscal Year: A company's accounting year. Due to the nature of particular businesses, some companies do not use the calendar year for their bookkeeping. A typical example is the department store which finds December 31 too early a date to close its books after the Christmas rush and so ends its fiscal year on January 31.

Fixed Asset: A tangible long-term asset such as land, building or machinery, held for use rather than for processing or resale. A **Balance Sheet** category.

Fixed Charges: A company's expenses, such as debt interest, which it has agreed to pay whether or not earned, and which are deducted from income before income taxes are calculated.

Fixed Income Securities: Securities that generate a predictable stream of interest or **dividend** income, such as **bonds**, **debentures** and **preferred shares**.

Flat: Means that the quoted market price of a bond or debenture is its total cost (as opposed to *and accrued interest* transactions). Bonds and debentures in default of interest trade flat.

Floor Trader: Employee of a member of a stock exchange, who executes buy and sell orders on the floor (trading area) of the exchange for the firm and its clients.

Flow-Through Shares: Tax deductions and credits, normally available only to a corporation, may flow through to owners of the corporation's flow-through shares. Canadian exploration and mining companies are able to issue such shares at a premium because investors are considered to be funding exploration and development costs and are therefore entitled to deduct these expenses from all other income.

Formula Investing: An investment technique. One formula calls for the shifting of funds from common shares to preferred shares or bonds as the stock market, on average, rises above a certain predetermined point – and the return of funds to common share investments as the stock market average declines.

Fully Diluted Earnings per Share: **Earnings per common share** calculated on the assumption that all **convertible** securities are converted into **common shares** and all outstanding **rights**, **warrants**, **options** and contingent issues are exercised.

Fundamental Analysis: Security analysis based on fundamental facts about a company – sales, earnings, **dividend** prospects. (See also **Technical Analysis**.)

Funded Debt: All outstanding bonds, debentures, notes and similar debt instruments of a company not due for at least one year.

General Mortgage Bond: A bond which is secured by a blanket mortgage on the company's property, but which is usually subordinated to one or more other mortgage bonds.

Gross-up and Credit System: A procedure to encourage Canadians to invest in **preferred** and **common shares** of taxable, dividend-paying Canadian corporations. Not available on **interest** from **bonds**. The taxpayer pays tax based on grossing up (i.e. adding 25% to the amount of **dividends** actually received and obtains a credit against federal and provincial tax based on the grossed up amount.

Growth Stock: **Common stock** of a company with excellent prospects for above-average growth; a company which over a period of time seems destined for above-average expansion.

GTC Order: Good till cancelled order. Same as **Open Order**.

Guaranteed Investment Certificate (GIC): A deposit instrument most commonly available from trust companies, requiring a minimum investment at a predetermined rate of **interest** for a stated term. Generally non-redeemable prior to maturity but there can be exceptions.

Hedge: A protective manoeuvre; a transaction intended to reduce the risk of loss from price fluctuations.

Holding Company: A company that owns the securities of another company, in most cases with voting control.

Hypothecate: To pledge securities as collateral for a loan.

If, as and when: New issues are sold before the security **certificates** are printed. This clause in the contract protects the dealer against delay in receiving the certificates.

In-and-Out: Purchase and sale of the same security within a short period – a day, week, even a month. An in-and-out trader is more interested in profiting from day-to-day price fluctuations than in **dividends** or long-term growth.

Income Bond: Generally, an income bond promises to repay principal but to pay **interest** only when earned. In some cases, unpaid interest on an income bond may accumulate as a claim against the company when the bond matures.

Income Stock: A stock that provides a generous **dividend** yield that is relatively well assured.

Index: See **Averages**.

Information Circular: Document sent to shareholders with a **proxy**, providing details of matters to come before a shareholders' meeting.

Insider: All directors and senior officers of a corporation and those who may also be presumed to have access to inside information concerning the company; also anyone owning more than 10% of the voting shares in a corporation.

Insider Report: A report of all transactions in the shares of a company by those considered to be insiders of the company and submitted each month to securities commissions.

Instalment Debentures: See **Serial Bond**.

Instalment Receipts: A new issue of stock sold with the obligation that buyers will pay the issue price in a specified series of instalment payments instead of one lump sum payment. (Also known as *Partially Paid Shares*.)

Intangible Asset: An **asset** having no physical substance (e.g. goodwill, patents, franchises, copyrights).

Interest: Money charged by a lender to a borrower for the use of the lent money.

Interim Certificate: When a new issue is marketed, initial delivery of temporary **certificates** is sometimes made, to be exchanged for permanent or definitive certificates when these become available.

Interim Statement: A financial statement issued for a period within a fiscal year, e.g. a three-month or first quarter interim statement.

Intrinsic Value: That portion of a **warrant, right,** or **call** option's price that represents the amount by which the **market price** of a security exceeds the price at which these securities may be exercised.

Inventory Turnover Ratio: Cost of goods sold divided by inventory. The ratio may also be expressed as the number of days required to sell current inventory by dividing the ratio into 365.

Investment: The use of money to make more money, to gain income or increase **capital** or both.

Investment Advisor: A salesperson employed by a securities firm who must be registered by the Securities Commission of the province in which they work.

Investment Company or Fund: A company which uses its capital to invest in other companies. There are two principal types: *closed-end* and *open-end* or *mutual* fund. Shares in closed-end investment companies are readily transferable in the open market and are bought and sold like other shares. Capitalization is fixed. Open-end funds sell their own new shares to investors, buy back their old shares, and are not listed. Open-end funds are so-called because their capitalization is not fixed; they normally issue more shares as people want them.

Investment Counsellor: A professional engaged to give investment advice on securities for a fee.

Investment Dealer: A securities firm or an individual associated with one. When underwriting new securities or in most bond trading, the dealer acts as a principal, owning the securities bought or sold.

Investor: One whose principal concern is the minimization of risk, in contrast to the speculator, who is prepared to accept calculated risk in the hope of making better-than-average profits, or the gambler, who is prepared to take even greater risks.

Issue: Any of a company's securities; the act of distributing such securities.

Issuer Bid: An offer by an issuer to security holders to buy back any of its own shares or other securities convertible into its shares.

Jitney: The execution and clearing of orders by one member of a stock exchange for the account of another member. Example: Broker A is a small firm whose volume of business is not sufficient to maintain a trader on the floor of the exchange. Instead it gives its orders to Broker B for execution and clearing and pays a reduced percentage of the normal commission.

Junior Bond Issue: A corporate **bond** issue, the collateral for which has been pledged as security for other more senior **debt** issues and is therefore subject to these prior claims.

Junior Debt: One or more **junior bond issues**.

Lagging Indicators: A selection of statistical data, that on average, indicate highs and lows in the business cycle *behind* the economy as a whole. These relate to business expenditures for new plant and equipment, consumers' instalment credit, short-term business loans, the overall value of manufacturing and trade inventories.

Leading Indicators: A selection of statistical data that, on average, indicate highs and lows in the business cycle *ahead* of the economy as a whole. These relate to employment, capital investment, business starts and failures, profits, stock prices, inventory adjustment, housing starts and certain commodity prices.

Leverage: The effect of fixed charges (i.e. debt interest or preferred dividends, or both) on per-share earnings of common stock. Increases or decreases in income before fixed charges result in magnified percentage increases or decreases in earnings per common share. Leverage also applies to seeking magnified percentage returns on an investment by using borrowed funds, margin accounts or securities which require payment of only a fraction of the underlying security's value (such as rights, warrants or options).

Leveraged Buy Out (LBO): A takeover financed to a large degree by debt that is secured, serviced and repaid through the cash flow and assets of the acquired company. Typically, an LBO is financed predominantly by bank debt and low quality (*junk*) bonds and to a minimum degree by equity. Its extreme **leverage** makes an LBO dependent upon a stable economy and stable interest rates for its success.

Liabilities: **Debts** or obligations of a company, usually divided into **current liabilities** – those due and payable within one year – and long-term liabilities – those payable after one year. A **Balance Sheet** category.

Limit Order: A client's order to a broker to buy or sell at a specific price or better. The order can be executed only at that price or a better one.

Limited Liability: The word *limited* at the end of a Canadian company's name implies that liability of the company's shareholders is limited to the money they paid to buy the shares. By contrast, ownership by a sole proprietor or partnership carries unlimited personal legal responsibility for **debts** incurred by the business.

Liquidation: The process of converting securities or other property into cash. When a company is dissolved, cash remaining after sale of its **assets** and payment of all **liabilities** is distributed to the **shareholders**.

Liquidity: 1. The ability of the market in a particular security to absorb a reasonable amount of buying or selling at reasonable price changes. 2. A corporation's **current assets** relative to its **current liabilities**; its cash position.

Listed Stock: The stock of a company which is traded on a stock exchange.

Listing Statement: A stock exchange document published when a company's shares are accepted for listing. It provides basic information on the company, its business, management, **assets**, **capitalization** and financial status.

Load: The portion of the offering price of shares of most open-end **investment companies** (mutual funds) which covers sales commissions and all other costs of distribution.

Locked In: When an investor has a profit on a security he owns but does not sell because of either the absence of a market or some legal restriction on the sale of the security. Also refers to an investor holding a security which has declined below the purchase price who cannot sell without incurring a loss.

Long: Signifies ownership of securities. "I am long 100 BCE common" means that the speaker owns 100 **common** shares of BCE Inc.

Long-Term Bond: A **bond** or **debenture** maturing in more than ten years.

Major Trend: Underlying price trend prevailing in a market despite temporary declines or rallies.

Managed Account: Similar to a **Discretionary Account** but more long-term in nature. May be solicited.

Manipulation: The illegal practice of buying or selling a security for the purpose of creating a false or misleading appearance of active trading or for the purpose of raising or depressing the price to induce purchases or sales by others.

Margin: The amount paid by a client when he uses credit to buy a security, the balance being loaned by the dealer against acceptable collateral.

Market Maker: A trader employed by a securities firm who is authorized and required by applicable self-regulatory organizations (**SRO**s) to maintain reasonable liquidity in securities markets by making firm **bids** or **offers** for one or more designated securities.

Market Order: An order placed to buy or sell a security immediately at the best current price.

Market Out Clause: A clause in an **underwriting** agreement allowing the underwriter to rescind the underwriting agreement without penalty for certain specified reasons, such as the issue becoming unsaleable due to an unexpected change in securities markets or in the affairs of the company whose securities are being underwritten.

Market Price: The most recent price at which a security transaction took place.

Marketable: Easily bought or sold.

Material Change: a change in the affairs of a company that is expected to have a significant effect on the market value of its securities.

Maturity: The date on which a loan or a **bond** or **debenture** comes due and is to be paid off.

Medium-Term Bond: A **bond** or **debenture** maturing in over three but less than ten years.

Member Firm: A stock brokerage firm or investment dealer which is a member of a stock exchange or the Investment Dealers Association of Canada.

Minority Interest: 1. The equity of the shareholders who do not hold controlling interest in a controlled company; 2. In Consolidated Financial Statements (i) the item in the **balance sheet** of the parent company representing that portion of the assets of a consolidated subsidiary considered as accruing to the shares of the subsidiary not owned by the parent; and (ii) the item deducted in the **earnings statement** of the parent and representing that portion of the subsidiary's earnings considered as accruing to the subsidiary's shares not owned by the parent.

Monetary Policy: A policy implemented by the federal government through the Bank of Canada to control credit and the money supply in the economy.

Money Market: That part of the capital market in which short-term financial obligations are bought and sold. These include **treasury bills** and other federal government securities maturing in three years or less and **commercial paper**, **bankers' acceptances**, trust company **guaranteed investment certificates** and other instruments with a year or less left to maturity. Longer term securities, when their term shortens to the limits mentioned, are also traded in the money market.

Mortgage: A contract specifying that certain property is pledged as security for a loan.

Mortgage Backed Securities: Similar to **bonds**, the current $5,000 units with five-year terms are backed by a share in a pool of home **mortgages** insured under the National Housing Act. Units pay **interest** and a part of **principal** each month and, if home owners prepay their mortgages, may pay out additional amounts of principal before normal **maturity**. They trade in the bond market at prices reflecting current interest rates.

Multiple: A colloquial term for the **price earnings** ratio of a company's **common** shares.

Mutual Fund: See **Investment Fund**.

Near Banks: See **Country Banks**.

Negative Pledge Provision: A protective provision written into the trust indenture of a company's **debenture** issue providing that no subsequent mortgage **bond** issue may be secured by all or part of the company's **assets**, unless at the same time the company's debentures are similarly secured.

Negotiable: A **certificate** that is transferable by delivery and which, in the case of a registered certificate, has been duly endorsed and guaranteed.

Net Asset Value: Total assets of a corporation less its **liabilities**. Also referred to as Shareholders' **Equity**.

Net Change: The change in the price of a security from the closing price on one day to the closing price on the following trading day. In the case of a stock which is entitled to a dividend one day, but is traded **ex-dividend** the next, the dividend is not considered in computing the change. The same applies to stock splits. A stock selling at $100 the day before a two-for-one split and trading the next day at $50 would be considered unchanged. The net change is ordinarily the last figure in a stock price list. The mark $+ 1^1/_8$ means up $1.125 a share from the last sale on the previous day the stock traded.

Net Earnings: That part of a company's profits remaining after all expenses and taxes have been paid and out of which **dividends** may be paid.

New Issue: An offering of stocks or **bonds** sold by a company for the first time. Proceeds may be used to retire outstanding securities of the company, to purchase **fixed assets** or for additional **working capital**. New **debt** issues are also offered by government bodies.

No Par Value (n.p.v.): Indicates a **common stock** has no stated face value.

Non-Cumulative: A preferred **dividend** which does not accrue or accumulate if unpaid.

Note: An unsecured promise to pay.

Odd Lot: A number of shares which is less than a **board lot**.

Off-the-Board: This term may refer to transactions over-the-counter in unlisted securities, or, in a special situation, to a transaction involving a block of listed shares which is not executed on a recognized stock exchange.

Offer: The lowest price at which a person is willing to sell; as opposed to **bid** which is the highest price at which one is willing to buy.

Of Record: On the company's books or record. If, for example, a company announces that it will pay a **dividend** to shareholders of record January 15, every shareholder whose name appears on the company's books on that day will be sent a dividend cheque from the company.

Open-End Fund: See **Investment Fund**.

Open Order: An order to buy or sell a security at a specified price, valid until executed or cancelled.

Option: A right to buy or sell specific securities or properties at a specified price within a specified time. (See **Puts and Calls**.)

Option Eligible Securities: Securities which meet the eligibility criteria as underlying securities for either Canadian (TransCanada Options – TCO) or U.S. (Options Clearing Corporation – OCC) exchange-traded put and call options. In Canada, option eligible securities, securities **convertible** into option eligible securities and **preferred** shares of companies whose securities qualify as option eligible securities, require minimum client **margin** (for purchase on margin) of 30% of their market value.

Out-of-Line: A security which appears to be selling too low or too high in relation to comparable issues.

Over-the-Counter (OTC): A market for securities made up of securities dealers who may or may not be members of a recognized stock exchange. Over-the-counter is mainly a market conducted over the telephone. Also called the *unlisted, inter-dealer* or *street market*.

Paper Profit: An unrealized profit on a security still held. Paper profits become realized profits only when the security is sold. A *paper loss* is the opposite to this.

Par Value: The stated face value of a bond or stock (as assigned by the company's charter) expressed as a dollar amount per share. Par value of a **common stock** usually has little relationship to the current market value and so *no par value* stock is now more common. Par value of a **preferred stock** is significant as it indicates the dollar amount of **assets** each preferred share would be entitled to should the company be liquidated.

Pari Passu: In equal proportion. Usually refers to equally ranking issues of a company's **preferred** shares.

Participating Feature: Some preferred shares which, in addition to their fixed rate of prior **dividend**, share with the **common** in further **dividend** distributions and in capital distributions above their **par value** in **liquidation**.

Penny Stocks: Low-priced speculative issues selling at less than $1 a share. Frequently used as a term of disparagement, although some penny stocks have developed into investment calibre issues.

Piggy Back Warrants: A second series of warrants acquired upon exercise of primary warrants sold as part of a unit.

Point: Refers to security prices. In the case of shares, it means $1 per share. In the case of **bonds** and **debentures**, it means 1% of the issue's par value which is almost universally 100. On a $1,000 bond, one point represents 1% of the face value of the bond or $10.

Poison Pill: A corporate provision to combat hostile takeovers. When triggered, the poison pill allows shareholders to acquire additional shares at below market price, thereby increasing the number of shares outstanding and making the takeover prohibitively expensive. These plans are the subject of some controversy regarding whom they are designed to protect.

Pooled Shares: See **Escrowed Shares**.

Pooling of Interest: Occurs when a company issues **treasury shares** for the **assets** of another company so that the latter becomes a division or subsidiary of the acquiring company. Subsequent accounts of the parent company are set up to include the **retained earnings** and assets at **book value** (subject to certain adjustments) of the acquired company.

Portfolio: Holdings of securities by an individual or institution. A portfolio may contain **debt** securities, **preferred** and **common stocks** of various types of enterprises and other types of securities.

Preferred Stock: A class of share capital that entitles the owners to a fixed **dividend** ahead of the company's **common** shares and to a stated dollar value per share in the event of **liquidation**. Usually do not have voting rights unless a stated number of dividends have been omitted.

Premium: The amount by which a **preferred stock** or **debt** security may sell above its **par value**. In the case of a new issue of **bonds** or stocks, the amount the market price rises over the original selling price. Also refers to that part of the redemption price of a bond or preferred share in excess of face value, par value or market price. In the case of **options**, the price paid by the buyer of an option contract to the seller.

Price Earnings Ratio: A common stock's current market price divided by its annual per share earnings.

Primary Distribution or Primary Offering of a New Issue: The original sale of any issue of a company's securities.

Prime Rate: The interest rate chartered banks charge to their most credit-worthy borrowers.

Principal: The person for whom a broker executes an order, or a dealer buying or selling for his own account. The term may also refer to a person's **capital** or to the face amount of a **bond**.

Prior Preferred: A preferred stock which in **liquidation** of the issuing company would rank ahead of other classes of preferred shares as to **asset** and **dividend** entitlement.

Private Placement: The **underwriting** of a security and its sale to a few buyers, usually institutional, in large amounts.

Pro Forma: A term applied to a document drawn up after giving effect to certain assumptions or contractual commitments not yet completed. For example, an issuer of new securities is required to include in the prospectus a statement of its **capitalization** on a pro forma basis after giving effect to the new financing.

Pro Rata: In proportion to. For example, a **dividend** is a pro rata payment because the amount of dividend each shareholder receives is in proportion to the number of shares he owns.

Profit Taking: Selling to take a profit – the process of converting **paper profits** into cash.

Program Trading: A sophisticated computerized trading strategy whereby a portfolio manager attempts to earn a profit from the price spreads between a portfolio of equities similar or identical to those underlying a designated stock index, e.g. the Standard & Poor 500

Index, and the price at which futures contracts (or their options) on the index trade in financial futures markets. Also refers to switching or trading blocks of securities in order to change the asset mix of a portfolio.

Prospectus: A legal document which describes securities being offered for sale to the public. Must be prepared in conformity with requirements of applicable securities commissions. (See **Draft Prospectus**, **Red Herring** and **Final Prospectus**.)

Proxy: Written authorization given by a shareholder to someone else, who need not be a shareholder, to represent him or her and vote his or her shares at a shareholders' meeting.

Prudent Man Rule: An investment standard. In some provinces, the law requires that a fiduciary, such as a trustee, may invest funds only in a list of securities designated by the province or the federal government. In other provinces, the trustee may invest in a security if it is one which an ordinary prudent man would buy if he were investing for the benefit of other people for whom he felt morally bound to provide. Most provinces apply the two standards.

Purchase and Resale Agreement: The method by which **country banks** lend temporarily idle funds to money market dealers. The country bank buys short-term securities from the money market dealer who agrees to repurchase the securities from the country bank at a higher price at a specified future date.

Purchase Fund: A fund set up by a company to retire through purchases in the market a specified amount of its outstanding **preferred** shares or **debt** if purchases can be made at or below a stipulated price.

Push-Out: During a stock **split**, the process of the **transfer agent** forwarding new shares directly to the registered holders of old share **certificates**, without the holders having to surrender these old shares. Both old and new shares henceforth have equal value.

Puts and Calls: Options which give the holder the right, but not the obligation, to sell or buy a fixed amount of a certain stock at a specified price within a specified time. A put gives the holder the right to sell the stock; a call the right to buy the stock. Puts are generally purchased by those who think a stock may go down; calls by those who expect a price increase. Puts and calls are also available on **bonds**, currencies, precious metals, futures contracts and stock indices.

Put-through: See **Cross on the Board**.

Quotation or Quote: The highest bid to buy and the lowest offer to sell a security at a given time. Example: A quote of 45¼ - 45½ means that 45¼ is the highest price a buyer will pay and 45½ the lowest price a seller will accept.

Rally: A brisk rise in the general price level of the market or in an individual stock.

Reaction: Temporary price weakness following a price upswing.

Real Estate Investment Trust (REIT): An investment trust that specializes in real estate related investments including **mortgages**, construction loans, land and real estate securities in varying combinations.

Real Interest Rate: The nominal rate of **interest** minus the percentage change in the Consumer Price Index (i.e. the rate of inflation).

Record Date: See **Shareholder of Record**.

Red Herring: A preliminary **prospectus** so called because certain information is printed in red ink around the border of the front page. It does not contain all the information found in the **final prospectus**. Its purpose: to ascertain the extent of public interest in an issue while it is being reviewed by a Securities Commission.

Redemption: The purchase of securities by the issuer at a time and price stipulated in the terms of the securities.

Redemption Price: The price at which **debt** securities or **preferred** shares may be redeemed, at the option of the issuing company.

Refinancing or Refunding: New **debt** securities are sold by a government or a company and the money is used to pay off existing loans. Object may be to save **interest** costs, extend the maturity of the loan, or both.

Registered Security: A security recorded on the books of a company in the name of the owner. It can be transferred only when the **certificate** is endorsed by the registered owner. Registered **debt** securities may be registered as to **principal** only or fully registered. In the latter case, **interest** is paid by cheque rather than by **coupons** attached to the certificate. (See also **Bearer Security**.)

Registered Tax Deferral Savings Plans: Government-approved savings plans (such as registered pension plans, registered retirement savings plans, and registered retirement income funds) in which funds contributed by individuals are tax-deductible within certain limits, and investment earnings accumulate in the plans tax-free until deregistration or maturity of the plans.

Registrar: Usually a trust company appointed by a company to prevent the over-issue of **common** or **preferred** shares. The registrar receives both the old cancelled **certificate** and the new certificate from the **transfer agent** and records and signs the new certificate. The registrar is, in effect, an auditor checking on the accuracy of the work of the transfer agent, although in most cases the registrar and transfer agent are the same trust company.

Registration: Before a public offering of new securities by a company or of outstanding securities by controlling stockholders may be made, the securities must be registered under the Securities Act of each province in which the securities will be offered. This usually involves filing a **Prospectus**.

Regular Delivery: Unless otherwise stipulated, sellers of stocks must deliver such shares by the fifth full **business day** after sale.

Reporting Issuer: Usually, a corporation that has issued or has outstanding securities that are held by the public and is subject to **continuous disclosure** requirements of securities administrators.

Restricted Shares: Shares that participate in a company's earnings and **assets** (in **liquidation**), as **common** shares do, but generally have restrictions on voting rights or else no voting rights.

Retained Earnings: The cumulative total of annual earnings retained by a company after payment of all expenses and **dividends**.

Retractable: A feature which can be included in a new **debt** or **preferred** issue, granting the holder the option under specified conditions to redeem the security on a stated date – prior to **maturity** in the case of a bond.

Reverse Split: The exchange of a greater number of a company's shares for a lesser number, e.g. one for three. Results in a higher share price and less shares outstanding. Same as a *Consolidation*.

Right: A short-term privilege granted to a company's **common** shareholders to purchase additional common shares, usually at a discount, from the company itself, at a stated price and within a specified time period. Rights of listed companies trade on stock exchanges from the ex rights date until their expiry.

Right of Rescission: The right of a purchaser of a new issue to rescind the purchase contract within the applicable time limits if the **prospectus** contained an untrue statement or omitted a material fact.

Right of Withdrawal: The right of a purchaser of a new issue to withdraw from the purchase agreement within two **business days** after receiving the **prospectus**.

Seat: The traditional term for membership on a stock exchange.

SEC: The Securities and Exchange Commission, a federal body established by the United States Congress, to protect investors in the U.S. In Canada there is no national regulatory authority; instead, securities legislation is provincially administered.

Secondary Distribution or Secondary Offering: The redistribution of a block of stock sometime after it has been sold by the issuing company. Usually a large block of shares is involved (e.g. from the settlement of an estate) and these are offered to the public at a fixed price, set in relationship to the stock's market price.

Securities Acts: Provincial Acts administered by the Securities Commission in each province, which set down the rules under which securities may be issued and traded.

Securities Administrator: A general term referring to the provincial regulatory authority (e.g. Securities Commission or Provincial Registrar) responsible for administering a provincial **Securities Act**.

Securities Advisor: A person or firm registered with applicable securities commissions to advise the public generally with regard to specific securities, often through publications.

Securitization: Refers in a narrow sense to the process of converting loans of various sorts into marketable securities by packaging the loans into pools. In a broader sense, refers to the development of markets for a variety of **debt** instruments that permit the ultimate borrower to bypass the banks and other deposit-taking institutions and to borrow directly from lenders.

Selling Group: Investment dealers or others who assist a banking group in marketing a new issue of securities without assuming financial liability if the issue is not entirely sold. The use of a selling group widens the distribution of a new issue.

Senior Bond Issue: A corporate bond issue which has priority over other bonds as to its claim on the company's **assets** and earnings. Example: first mortgage bond.

Senior Debt: One or more senior **bond** issues.

Serial Bond or Debenture: A **bond** or **debenture** issue in which a predetermined amount of **principal** matures each year.

Settlement Date: The date on which a securities buyer must pay for a purchase or a seller must deliver the securities sold. For most securities, settlement must be made on or before the fifth **business day** following the **transaction date**.

Short Sale: The sale of a security which the seller does not own. This is a speculative practice done in the belief that the price of a stock is going to fall and the seller will then be able to cover the sale by buying it back later at a lower price, thereby making a profit on the transactions. It is illegal for a seller not to declare a short sale at the time of placing the order.

Short-term Bond: A **bond** or **debenture** maturing within three years.

Short-term Debt: Company borrowings repayable within one year that appear in the **current liabilities** section of the corporate **Balance Sheet.** The most common short-term debt items are: bank advances or loans, notes payable and the portion of funded debt due within one year.

Sinking Fund: A fund set up to retire most or all of a **debt** or **preferred** share issue over a period of time.

Speculator: One who is prepared to accept calculated risks in the marketplace. Objectives are usually short to medium-term capital gain, as opposed to regular income and safety of **principal**, the prime objectives of the conservative investor.

Split: The division of a company's outstanding **common** shares into a larger number of common shares. A three-for-one split by a company with one million common shares outstanding would result in three million common shares outstanding after the split. Each holder of 100 common shares before the split would receive 200 additional common shares. Each common shareholder's proportionate interest in the company remains the same.

Spread: The gap between **bid** and asked prices in the quotation for a security. Also a term used in Option trading.

SRO: Short for Self Regulatory Organization such as the Investment Dealers Association of Canada and the principal stock exchanges.

Statement of Changes in Financial Position: A financial statement which provides information as to how a company generated and spent its cash during the year. Assists users of financial statements in evaluating the company's ability to generate cash internally, repay **debts**, reinvest and pay **dividends** to shareholders.

Statement of Material Facts: A document presenting the relevant facts about a company and compiled in connection with an **underwriting** or **secondary distribution** of its shares. It is used only when the shares underwritten or distributed are listed on a recognized stock exchange and takes the place of a **prospectus** in such cases.

Stock Dividend: A pro rata payment to **common** shareholders of additional common stock. Such payment increases the number of shares each holder owns but does not alter a shareholder's proportional ownership of the company.

Stop Buy and Stop Loss Orders: Orders to buy or sell, placed above or below the market price, which become **market orders** as soon as the price of a **board lot** of the stock rises or falls to the specified price. A stop buy order is used to protect against losses in a **short sale**, whereas a stop loss order may be used to protect a **paper profit** or to limit a possible loss when shares are already owned. Since such orders become market orders when the stop price is reached, there is no certainty they will be executed at that price.

Street Certificate: A stock certificate registered in the name of an investment dealer or stock broker in order to increase its negotiability, but beneficially owned by someone else.

Street Name: Securities registered in the name of a dealer, instead of the real or beneficial owner.

Strip Bonds or **Zero Coupon Bonds**: Usually high quality federal or provincial government **bonds** originally issued in bearer form, where some or all of the **interest coupons** have been detached. The bond **principal** and any remaining coupons (the *residue*) then trade separately from the strip of detached coupons, both at substantial discounts from par.

Stripped Debentures: Debentures which have been separated from other securities such as **warrants** which, together with the debentures, were originally issued together as a **unit**.

Subject Bid; Subject Offer: A **bid** or **offer** made for a security that indicates the buyer's interest in the case of a bid and the seller's interest in the case of an offer, but does not commit the bidder or offeror to the purchase or sale of the security at that price or time.

Subsidiary: Company which is controlled by another company usually through its ownership of the majority of shares.

Sweetener: A feature included in the terms of a new issue of **debt** or **preferred** shares to make the issue more attractive to initial investors. Examples include **warrants** and/or **common** shares sold with the issue as a **unit** or a **convertible** or **extendible** or **retractable** feature.

Switching: Selling one security and buying another.

Syndicate: A group of investment dealers who together underwrite and distribute a new issue of securities or a large block of an outstanding issue.

Take-Over Bid: An offer made to security holders of a company to purchase voting securities of the company which, with the offeror's already owned securities, will in total exceed 20% of the outstanding voting securities of the company. For federally incorporated companies, the equivalent requirement is more than 10% of the outstanding voting shares of the target company.

Talon: A coupon or a **certificate** similar to a **warrant**, attached to another security and carrying some right or privilege.

T-Bills: A colloquialism for government **treasury bills**.

Technical Analysis (Charting): A method of market and security analysis that studies investor attitudes and psychology as revealed in charts of stock price movements and trading volumes. Object: to predict future price action.

Term Deposit Receipt: A deposit instrument most commonly available from chartered banks, requiring a minimum investment at a predetermined rate of **interest** for a stated term. The interest rate varies according to the amount invested and the term to **maturity** but is competitive with comparable alternative investments. A reduced interest rate usually applies if funds are withdrawn prior to maturity.

Thin Market: A market in which there are comparatively few **bids** to buy or **offers** to sell or both. The phrase may apply to a single security or to the entire stock market. In a thin market, price fluctuations between transactions are usually larger than when the market is liquid. A thin market in a particular stock may reflect lack of interest in that issue, or a limited supply of the stock.

Time Value: The amount, if any, by which the current market price of a **right**, **warrant** or **option** exceeds its **Intrinsic Value**.

Timely Disclosure: An obligation imposed by securities administrators on companies, their officers and directors to release promptly to the news media any favourable or unfavourable corporate information which is of a material nature. Broad dissemination of this news allows non-insiders to trade the company's securities with the same knowledge about the company as insiders themselves. (See also **Continuous Disclosure**.)

Trader: Employee of a securities firm who executes buy and sell orders for the firm and its clients either on a stock exchange or the OTC market. Also a client who buys and sells frequently with the objective of short-term profit.

Transaction Date: The date on which the purchase or sale of a security takes place.

Transfer Agent: A trust company appointed by a company to keep a record of the names, addresses and number of shares held by its shareholders. Frequently, the transfer agent also distributes **dividend** cheques.

Treasury Bills: Short-term government debt issued in denominations ranging from $1,000 to $1,000,000. Treasury bills do not pay **interest**, but are sold at a discount and mature at par (100% of face value). The difference between the purchase price and par at maturity represents the lender's (purchaser's) income in lieu of interest. In Canada such gain is taxed as interest income in the purchaser's hands.

Treasury Shares: Authorized but unissued stock of a company or previously issued shares that have been re-acquired by the corporation.

Trustee: For bondholders, usually a trust company appointed by the company to protect the security behind the **bonds** and to make certain that all covenants of the trust deed relating to the bonds are honoured.

Two Way Security: A security, usually a **debenture** or **preferred share**, which is **convertible** into or exchangeable for another security (usually **common** shares) of the same company. Also indirectly refers to the possibility of profiting in the future from upward movements in the underlying common shares as well as receiving in the interim **interest** or **dividend** payments.

Underwriting: The purchase for resale of a security issue by one or more investment dealers or *underwriters*. The formal agreements pertaining to such a transaction are called *underwriting agreements*.

Unit: Two or more corporate securities (such as **preferred shares** and **warrants**) offered for sale to the public at a single, combined price.

Unlisted: A security not listed on a stock exchange but traded on the **over-the-counter** market.

Value Date: See **Settlement Date**.

Voting Right: The stockholder's right to vote in the affairs of his company. Most **common** shares have one vote each. **Preferred stock** usually has the right to vote only when its **dividends** are in arrears. The right to vote may be delegated by the shareholder to another person. (See **Proxy**.)

Voting Trust: An arrangement to place the control of a company in the hands of certain managers for a given period of time, or until certain results have been achieved, by shareholders surrendering their voting rights to a **trustee** for a specified period of time.

Warrant: A **certificate** giving the holder the right to purchase securities at a stipulated price within a specified time limit. Warrants are usually issued with a new issue of securities as an inducement or **sweetener** to investors to buy the new issue.

When Issued: Indicates a conditional transaction in a security authorized for issuance, but not as yet actually issued.

Working Capital: **Current assets** minus **current liabilities**. This figure is an indication of the company's ability to meet its short-term **debts**.

Working Capital Ratio: **Current assets** of a company divided by its **current liabilities**.

Working Control: Theoretically ownership of 51% of a company's voting stock is necessary to exercise control. In practice – and this is particularly true in the case of a large corporation – effective control sometimes can be exerted through ownership, individually or by a group acting in concert, of less than 50%.

Wrap Account: Also known as a wrap fee program. A type of fully **discretionary account** where a single annual fee, based on the account's total **assets**, is charged, instead of **commissions** and advice and service charges being levied separately for each transaction. The account is then managed separately from all other wrap accounts, but is kept consistent with a model portfolio suitable to clients with similar objectives.

Yield - Bond & Stock: Return on an investment. A stock yield is calculated by expressing the annual **dividend** as a percentage of the current market price of the stock. A bond yield is a more complicated calculation, involving annual **interest** payments plus **amortizing** the difference between its current market price and **par value** over the life of the bond. This yield can be obtained from a bond yield table or from a computer.

Yield Curve: The relationship among the yields of **bonds** of the same quality but different maturities, put into graphic form.

Zero Coupon Bonds: See **Strip Bonds**.

Bibliography

This list is far from exhaustive and should merely serve as a guide. Many of the books contain bibliographies which will suggest other works. Some of the books may be out of print but still available in libraries. A maple leaf ❦ before an entry denotes a Canadian publication.

Investments and Investing

❦ Hugh Anderson, *Bulls And Bears*, Financial Times Library, Penguin Books

R. Badger, H. Torgeson and H. Gulhmann, *Investment Principles and Practices*, Prentice-Hall Inc.

J. Clendenin and G. Christy, *Introduction to Investments*, McGraw Hill

J. Cohen, E. Zinbarg and A. Zeikel, *Guide to Intelligent Investing*, Dow-Jones Irwin

—, *Investment Analysis and Portfolio Management*, Fifth edition, Dow-Jones Irwin

Sidney Cottle, Roger F. Murray and Frank E. Block with the collaboration of Martin L. Leibowitz, *Graham and Dodd's Security Analysis*, Fifth Edition, McGraw-Hill, New York

H. Dougall, *Investments*, Prentice-Hall Inc.

C. Ellis, *Institutional Investing*, The Ronald Press Co.

Benjamin Graham, *The Intelligent Investor*, Harper & Bros.

♣ A. Granger, *Investing Profitably in Canada*, J. J. Douglas Ltd. (Available in paperback)

♣ James E. Hatch and Michael J. Robinson, *Investment Management in Canada*, 2nd edition, Prentice-Hall

Frank K. Reilly, *Investments*, Dryden Press

C. J. Rols and G.J. Nelson, *The Anatomy of Wall Street*, Lippincott Publishing

W.F. Sharpe, G.J. Alexander and D.J. Fowler, *Investments,* Prentice Hall

L. Wright, *Principles of Investments* – Text and Cases, Grid Publishing Inc.

♣ Henry B. Zimmer, *The New Canadian Tax & Investment Guide for Executives, Professionals & Business*, Hurtig Publishers Ltd.

Accounting

D. F. Hawkins, *Corporate Financial Reporting*, Dow-Jones Irwin

♣ J. Langhout, *Analysis and Interpretation of Canadian Financial Statements*, University Press of Canada

♣ Pyle, White and Zin, *Fundamental Accounting Principles*, Irwin-Dorsey Limited

Economics

♣ M. Archer, *Introduction to Economics, A Canadian Analysis*, Maurice Archer Enterprises Inc., Oakville, Ontario

G. Haberlen, *Inflation, Its Causes and Cures*, American Enterprise Institute For Public Policy Research

H. Hazlitt, *Economics in One Lesson*, Harper & Bros.

♣ Peter Martin, *Inside the Bank of Canada's Weekly Financial Statistics: A Technical Guide,* The Fraser Institute

♣ C. R. McConnell and W. H. Pope, *Economics*, McGraw-Hill Ryerson Limited

♣ Paul Samuelson, *Economics*, 3rd Canadian edition, McGraw-Hill Ryerson Limited

Specialized Texts and Studies

Robin Amlot, *Dawn Traders' Guide to World Markets*, Boxtree Limited

❦ M. Archer, *Introduction to Canadian Business*, McGraw-Hill Ryerson Limited

❦ Lloyd Besant (ed.), *Selected Papers of the Fourth and Fifth Canadian International Futures Conferences and Research Seminars*, The Canadian Securities Institute

J. A. Boeckh and R. T. Coghlan (ed.), *The Stock Market and Inflation*, Dow-Jones Irwin

❦ *The Canadian Trust Industry*, Trust Companies Institute of Canada, McGraw-Hill Ryerson

J. F. Childs, *Long Term Financing*, Prentice-Hall Inc.

Commodity Trading Manual, Chicago Board of Trade

Commodity Year Books, Commodity Research Bureau, New York

❦ John E. Hore, *Trading on Canadian Futures Markets*, 5th edition, Canadian Securities Institute

❦ W. T. Hunter, *Canadian Financial Markets*, Broadview Press (paperback)

G. L. Letter, The Stock Market, The Ronald Press Co.

Robert W. Kolb, *Financial Derivatives*, Prentice Hall

❦ Peter Martin, *Inside the Bank of Canada's Weekly Financial Statistics: A Technical Guide,* The Fraser Institute, Vancouver

Lawrence G. McMillan, *Options as a Strategic Investment,* New York Institute of Finance

❦ P. E. McQuillan, *Going Public in Canada – The Facts and the Fads*, The Canadian Institute of Chartered Accountants

Donald T. Mesler, *Warrants, Analysis and Investment Strategy*, Probus Publishing Company

❦ E. P. Neufeld, *The Financial System of Canada,* Macmillan of Canada

❧ S. Sarpkaya, *The Money Market in Canada*, Butterworth & Co. (Canada) Ltd.

❧ S. Taube, *Estate and Tax Planning*, The Carswell Company Limited

❧ Joanne T. Yaccato, *Balancing Act*, Prentice Hall

Your Guide to Going Public, B. C. Securities Commission

Popular Reading

Bernard Baruch, *My Own Story*, Holt Rinehart and Winston (paperback)

H. Black,*The Watchdogs of Wall Street*, Morrow Publishing

❧ Kathleen H. Brown, *Personal Finance for Canadians* 5th edition, Prentice Hall (paperback)

❧ David Chilton, *The Wealthy Barber*, Stoddart (paperback)

Deloitte & Touche, *Canadian Guide to Personal Financial Management,* 8th edition, Prentice Hall (paperback)

❧ John De Mont and Tracy Le May, *Guide to Mutual Funds*, Random House

J. K. Galbraith, *The Affluent Society*, Houghton

—, *The Great Crash-1929*, Pelican Books (available in paperback)

❧ *How To Be Sure You Get The Right R.R.S.P.*, MacLean-Hunter Ltd. (paperback)

G. M. Loeb, *The Battle for Investment Survival*, Simon & Schuster (available in paperback)

Peter Lynch, *One Up on Wall Street*, Simon & Schuster (available in paperback)

—, *Beating the Street,* Simon & Schuster

Charles MacKay, *Extraordinary Popular Delusions and the Madness of Crowds*, Farrar Straus and Girous (available in paperback)

❧ *Money Management*, MacLean-Hunter Ltd. (paperback)

H. B. Neill, *The Art of Contrary Thinking*, The Caxton Printers

✤ David Olive, *Just Rewards, The Case for Ethical Reform in Business*, Key Porter Books

✤ Gordon Pape, *Building Wealth in the '90s,* Prentice Hall

✤ —, *Low-Risk Investing*, Prentice Hall

✤ W. Reddins, *Successful Spending, Saving and Investing*, McGraw-Hill

Jack D. Schwager, *The New Market Wizards,* Harper Collins (paperback)

Adam Smith, *The Money Game*, Random House (available in paperback)

—, *The Roaring '80s*, Penguin (paperback)

—, *Supermoney*, Random House

R. Sobel, *Panic on Wall Street*, MacMillan Publishing

Through the Mutual Funds Maze, Grosvenor House Press Inc.

✤ Graydon G. Watters, *Financial Pursuit*, FKI Financial Knowledge Inc.

✤ *Your Guide To Investing For Bigger Profits*, MacLean-Hunter Ltd.

✤ *Your Money: How To Make The Most Of It*, MacLean-Hunter Ltd.

✤ Henry Zimmer, *Making Your Money Grow*, Collins (paperback)

SUPPLEMENTAL READINGS

THE FINANCIAL PRESS

Newspapers

✤ *The Financial Post* – 333 King Street East, Toronto, M5A 4N2, (416) 350-6507 - publishes a daily edition Tuesday to Friday and a weekly edition Saturday and contains summaries of Canadian and foreign markets, detailed industry studies and numerous articles on major political and economic events.

✤ *The Financial Times of Canada* – 440 Front Street West, Toronto M5V 3E6, (416) 585-5555 – published weekly covering many of the same topics.

♣ *The Globe and Mail* Report on Business – 444 Front Street West, Toronto M5V 2S9, (416) 585-5222 – published daily, Monday to Saturday.

♣ *Les Affaires* – 9th floor, 465 rue Saint-Jean, Montreal H2Y 3S4 – published weekly.

Two of the better known American financial papers are:

The Wall Street Journal – 200 Burnett Road, Chicopee, Mass. 01020 – published daily Monday to Friday.

Barrons – 200 Burnett Road, Chicopee, Mass. 01020 – published weekly.

Periodicals

♣ *Canadian Business* – 777 Bay Street, Toronto M5W 1A7 (416) 596-5100 – a general business magazine published monthly.

♣ *Canadian Investment Review* – 777 Bay Street, Toronto M5W 1A7 (416) 596-5000 – published quarterly.

♣ *The Northern Miner* – 1450 Don Mills Road, Don Mills M3B 2X7, (416) 445-6641 – published in tabloid newspaper form weekly and specializing in the mining industry.

♣ *Investor's Digest of Canada* – 133 Richmond Street West, Toronto M5H 3M8, (416) 869-1177 – published semi-monthly, it contains research reports on the stock market generally and specific companies and industries.

There are many American business magazines, a few of which are:

Business Week – Suite 32A, 70 Yorkville Avenue, Toronto M5R 1B9, (416) 926-8255 – published weekly.

Money – 541 North Fairbanks Court, Chicago, Illinois 60611 – a consumer magazine published monthly.

Fortune – 541 North Fairbanks Court, Chicago, Illinois 60611 – published monthly.

Futures – 250 South Wacker Drive, Suite 1150, Chicago, Illinois 60606 (312) 977-0999 – news, analysis and strategies for derivatives traders and money managers; published monthly.

Bank of Canada Publications - Bank of Canada, 234 Wellington Street, Ottawa, Ontario K1A 0G9, (613) 782-8248

❧ *Weekly Financial Statistics* – which covers the volume and yields of treasury bills sold at the weekly auctions; reports on government securities yields, interest rates in financial markets generally; and gives data on total government direct and guaranteed debt outstanding, balances of the Bank of Canada and the chartered banks, and foreign exchange reserves.

❧ *Bank of Canada Review* – a quarterly publication containing current and historic information and charts on the positions of the Bank of Canada and the chartered banks; information on federal, provincial and municipal debt issued and outstanding, market prices and yields, foreign exchange statistics, international flows of funds and a wide range of articles and economic statistics including the national accounts. Press releases issued by the Bank and speeches given by the Governor and other senior officials are also reprinted in the Review.

❧ *The Annual Report of the Governor* – which is directed to the Minister of Finance and contains a summary of the year's economic highlights and a description of the Bank's reaction to events.

Statistics Canada Publications – 25 St. Clair Avenue East, Toronto M4T 1M4, (416) 973-8018.

The federal government's statistical output emanates from Statistics Canada, the national central statistical agency which collects, compiles and publishes statistical data relating to a wide variety of economic and social activities in Canada. It issues an annotated *Catalogue of Current Publications,* available on request, which supplies a catalogue number, title, frequency, price, number of pages, and a brief annotation outlining th e contents of each report and the dates covered. There is a subject index showing the Statistics Canada publication in which statistical information on different subjects or commodities is to be found. There is also an index by title.

Other useful publications include a *Daily* and a *Weekly Bulletin,* containing news summaries and an announcement of Statistics Canada reports, as well as *The Canadian Statistical Review,* a monthly summary of current economic indicators in Canada showing monthly or quarterly statistics for at least the past two years. It contains a large number of tables of basic statistics and also a special section of many seasonally-adjusted major indicators and charts on significant data. Also featured are articles on general economic conditions and on special subjects.

Stock Exchange Publications

Informative monthly bulletins are published by the Toronto, Montreal, Alberta and Vancouver Exchanges, These Reviews give, for each exchange respectively, price ranges, volume, ticker symbol, dividend, number of authorized and outstanding shares, etc. of all listed securities; information on trading units; charts on Stock Market Indices; details of new listings, underwritings, options, rights, block trades and short positions; and informative articles on companies whose securities are listed as well as economic and market commentaries.

Securities Commission Bulletins

Informative *Bulletins* are published weekly under the authority of securities commissions in British Columbia, Alberta, Ontario and Quebec. They contain a broad range of information on commission policies, rulings, cease trading orders, trading reports of corporate insiders and details of a registration, new issues and secondary financing, take-over bids, issuer bids and continuous disclosure filings.

Securities Firm Publications

Most Canadian securities firms have a research staff (ranging from a single analyst up to 10-15 in some of the larger houses) to study industries, companies, municipalities and related securities. The purpose of their research is to select suitable securities for clients and advise them of appropriate times to buy and sell. Securities firms publish some of their findings in monthly investment letters and special industry and company reports for clients and other interested parties.

Information is also provided by independent investment counselling firms (as distinct from securities firms) but usually only to their clients and not to the general public.

The Financial Post DATAGROUP – 333 King Street East, Toronto M5A 4N2, (416) 350-6507.

Financial Post Surveys

The Financial Post DATAGROUP publishes an annual *Survey of Industrials,* a useful reference book which provides vital facts on over 6,000 Canadian publicly-owned corporations plus their subsidiaries and affiliates. Each public corporation is surveyed and information is given on the location of its head office, its transfer agent, a synopsis of its operations, names and locations of directors, its capitalization and details of its funded debt. Financial statistics from the company's balance sheet and earnings statement for the latest two years are also given. A review of major Canadian mutual funds is also provided.

A Survey of Mines and Energy Resources is published annually, providing coverage of more than 4,000 companies engaged in the Canadian natural resources industry.

The *Survey of Predecessor and Defunct Companies* is a record of changes to Canadian public corporations covering more than 50 years, with details of name changes, amalgamations and acquisitions covering some 12,000 corporate entities. Also included is information on companies being wound up or dissolved, and companies whose charters have been cancelled or struck from provincial registers.

These three surveys form the *Canadian Corporate Directories* which together cover most Canadian public companies.

Financial Post Investment Reports

These reports provide more detailed information on 500 Canadian public companies than do the *Surveys. Historical Reports* contain a detailed description and history of the company profiled; management, operations and capitalization details; plus seven years of company financial statements and a trading history dating back to the company's incorporation.

Investor Reports provide the latest reported trading and financial data, analysis, investment recommendations and ratings, material changes and ratios for all 500 companies in the Historical Reports.

Industry Reports offer a broader study of all 19 industries in which these 500 companies compete. Each Report ranks the leading companies in the industry according to revenue, summarizes their latest quarterly results, and presents seven years of industry ratios for trend analysis.

In addition to the *Financial Post Reports,* other services include the *Dividend Record* which is a record of dividends declared, stock splits or consolidations, name changes, redemption announcements and rights offerings. The Dividend Record is issued monthly with weekly supplements. An annual edition is also published.

Other publications include *Preferred Shares & Warrants,* which contains a listing of warrants and preferred shares, including retractable and convertible share issues. The *Government Bond Record* provides an extensive listing of Canadian federal and provincial outstanding debt securities. The *Corporate Bond Record* covers outstanding Canadian corporate debt, including convertible, retractable and extendible debt securities.

Investment Dealers Association of Canada Publications – Suite 1600, 121 King Street West, Toronto M5H 3T9, (416) 364-6133

The IDA publishes a Membership Directory and an IDA report three times yearly outlining developments in the securities industry and current Association activities. The IDA Bulletin, published quarterly, provides statistical information. Periodic economic outlooks and investment assessments are also available.

Northern Miner Press Limited Publications – 1450 Don Mills Road, Don Mills M3B 2X7, (416) 445-6641

The *Canadian Mines Handbook* is published annually by the Northern Miner Press Limited. It is a convenient and much-used reference book on Canadian mining companies and provides information on properties, development, financial condition, etc. It also provides mining share price ranges for 6 to 7 years, maps of mining areas, and further details on producing mines and mills.

The Northern Miner Press also publishes the *Canadian Oil and Gas Handbook* which contains information such as the development of properties, financial condition of companies, share price ranges and other information relating to oil and gas companies in Canada.

The Globe and Mail – 444 Front Street West, Toronto M5V 2S9, (416) 585-5222

Canada Company Handbook, published by Info Globe, the electronic publishing division of The Globe and Mail, provides information on many Canadian companies.

FRI Corporation, 1801 McGill College Avenue, Suite 600, Montreal, Quebec H3A 2N4, (514) 842-8809

The Canadian Government Bond Register - contains comprehensive information on the terms and conditions of all debt issued by federal and provincial governments and their agencies. Published in January and July.

Index

Many of these words also appear in the Glossary. As the glossary is alphabetic it has not been included in this index.